DODIE GOES SHOPPING
AND OTHER ADVENTURES

St. Martin's Press 🐏 *New York*

Dodie goes Shopping

and Other Adventures

DODIE KAZANJIAN

ILLUSTRATED BY CHESLEY McLAREN

The following essays originally appeared, in somewhat different form, in *Vogue*: "The Face," June 1997; "The Ball Gown," March 1998; "Thighs," May 1995; "The Fur Coat," November 1997; "Color," November 1998; "The Body," July 1997; "Long Hair," March 1999; "Calming Me Down," March 1999.

Book design by Gretchen Achilles
Illustrations by Chesley McLaren

Library of Congress Cataloging-in-Publication Data

Kazanjian, Dodie.
    Dodie goes shopping / Dodie Kazanjian. — 1st ed.
       p.   cm.
    ISBN 0-312-20528-7
    1. Kazanjian, Dodie, Anecdotes.   2. Fashion editors—United States Biography.   3. Women periodical editors—United States Biography.   4. Shopping.   5. Fashion.   6. Beauty, Personal. I. Title.
TT505.K375A3   1999
746.9'2'092—dc21
[B]   99-33895
                                                 CIP

FIRST EDITION: NOVEMBER 1999

10 9 8 7 6 5 4 3 2 1

Again, for Tad

CONTENTS

ACKNOWLEDGMENTS

I am especially grateful to Anna Wintour for her clear, smart, no-nonsense guidance and friendship. My thanks also to the wise editors at *Vogue* who have set me straight—Shelley Wanger, Katherine Betts, Mary Murray, Michael Boodro, Charles Gandee, Kristin van Ogtrop, Amy Astley, Wendy Hirschberg, and Joanne Chen—and to Jeffrey Frank at the *New Yorker*. To all those trendsetters who have inspired and informed my shopping—Brooke Hayward, Belle Coolidge, Adele Chatfield-Taylor, Eric Boman, Roxana Robinson, Gabriella Di Ferrari, and Dana Buckley—endless gratitude. Thank you, Wendy Sonnenberg, for your humor and honesty about femme fatalism. Thanks also to Sylvia Jukes Morris and her radar-like antennae for catching so many bloopers. Special thanks to Sally Richardson for wanting this book and to my agents and friends, Andrew Wylie and Jeffrey Posternak. It was a pleasure to work with Jennifer Enderlin, my editor at St. Martin's, and with Steve Snider, the very able art director there. I am grateful to Chesley McLaren for her witty and stylish drawings and to Charles Churchward for his creative guidance. This book was lucky enough to benefit from the legendary eye and council of my dear friend Alexander Liberman.

DODIE GOES SHOPPING

AND OTHER ADVENTURES

INTRODUCTION

I grew up in Newport, Rhode Island, where no one is supposed to grow up. Did you live in a mansion? people ask, thinking of those vast piles that so appalled Henry James when he revisited the town in the 1890s and found a "mere breeding ground for white elephants." In the first place, as any old-time Newporter knows, you never say "mansion." Even if you're talking about the Marble House or the Breakers, the word is "cottage." And no, I didn't live in one. I grew up in my grandfather's big old neo-Gothic house on Kay Street, built long before the cottages. But my grandfather helped to shape the ambience of the white elephants on Bellevue Avenue. The family firm, John H. Kazanjian & Co., imported the finest Chinese porcelains, antique carpets, furniture, and objets d'art and advised on matters of taste, which, among the new-rich Vanderbilts and Astors, was often in short supply.

In those days, before income tax, people thought nothing of giving ten-course dinners, or spending two hundred thousand turn-of-the-century dollars for a party on the lawn. Enormous tents were pitched outside houses choked with alabaster and porphyry, and platforms were constructed and fitted out with forty or fifty Oriental rugs and hundreds of handwoven

Chinese wicker chairs—all rented from John H. Kazanjian & Co. The firm was a landmark on Bellevue Avenue, in the center of town. Its Tudor-style building was designed by Richard Morris Hunt in the 1870s, shortly before Stanford White did the Newport Casino next door. The family business closed when my father died in 1966, and the building is now given over to boutiques that I never visit.

I can't forget the feeling of that old store, inside and out. A block long and three stories high, it was built originally as a hotel for bachelors. There was a sense of great style about the place, with its red brick and dark green timber facade and its green awnings stretching down Bellevue Avenue. Inside, you were in another world, another time. It was like a museum. One entrance placed you in the porcelain department, which was filled from floor to ceiling with seventeenth- and eighteenth-century Chinese vases, many of them taller than I was. (Most of the objects had been brought out of China before the turn of the century by my father's father, who started the business in 1880.) As a child, I used to keep my arms straight at my sides, for fear of knocking something over. An old Newport friend of mine says he felt like he was "entering Ali Baba's cave" every time he went there. The wooden floor creaked, and the place was full of rich but indefinable scents and memories. In aisle after aisle, jammed on shelves that reached up to the ceiling, was an eclectic mix of fabulous objects—Japanese lacquer boxes, carved jade animals, hand-made toys, Indian silks and textiles, archaic bronzes, and acres of Chinese export plates, platters, bowls, tureens, and tea services.

All of this may help to explain why there's such an eclectic mix of subjects in this book. Most of the pieces have appeared in *Vogue* magazine during the last two years, and some of them might not seem to belong in a book on shopping. For example, my story on the femme fatale, or the one on the WASP hotel. But why not go shopping for an antique vacation or a new personality, even if you're not going to adopt it? Shopping is at least 50 percent fantasy, as I discovered in Ali Baba's cave. We buy the stuff we need, like food and Kleenex, but there's another level of shopping, where we're engaged in a quest for things that will change our life or redefine who we are—the odd, the exotic, the original, the one-of-a-kind bounties that hardly ever turn up but are so thrilling when they do. Whether it's thinner thighs or stress reduction or a Cinderella ball gown by Badgley Mischka, we should pursue them with skepticism as well as ardor, because the ideal (what we're really after here) is the ultimate fantasy.

A part of me still haunts the quiet aisles of that store on Bellevue Avenue. My latest find, at a New York City flea market, is a pair of nineteenth-century carved rosewood Chinese lanterns, which I can't wait to rehabilitate—they need to be electrified and refitted with Chinese rice paper on the sides. The lanterns match the rosewood fire screen I rescued from my mother's house in Newport. I'm almost positive that when I get them right, my life will be perfect—for a few hours, anyway.

The Face

Andy Warhol once said that an artist is "somebody who produces things that people don't need to have, but that he—for some reason—thinks it would be a good idea to give them."

That's how I used to feel about cosmetic surgeons. Maybe

fashion models or movie stars could justify their face jobs on professional grounds, but for the rest of us, it was just vanity, self-indulgence, and a crime against nature.

But then I turned forty. Right on cue, two sets of facial lines made their unwelcome appearance, up there between my eyebrows and on either side of my smile. Friends began telling me I looked tired. And I found myself reading articles about face-lifts, brow-lifts, breast-lifts, breast reductions, abdomen tucks, chemical peels, implants, liposuction, laser surgery, and all the other "atrocities" (as my husband calls them) that were constantly turning up in magazines. The stuff horrified me and fascinated me in about equal measure.

To a certain extent, you could say I had a proprietary interest in the subject. A relative of mine, Dr. Varaztad Kazanjian, pioneered the techniques of modern plastic surgery and wrote a textbook that is considered the bible in that field. I remember visiting him in his Boston office when I was ten; he was tiny (like all Kazanjians), with a thick mop of white hair and a substantial Armenian nose that nobody would ever have wanted to tamper with. He had made his name as a battlefield surgeon during World War I, reconstructing faces that had been shattered by bullets or schrapnel. But because he died in 1974, I don't know how he would have felt about collagen injections and nipple-lifts. All I know is that my curiosity about the whole business had been mounting, to the point where I decided to talk with several plastic surgeons, to see what they thought I should do, if anything, about my fleeting youth.

Since I'm a sucker for name brands—my Chanel suit, my Kelly bag from Hermès, my Armani jacket, my Manolo Blahnik mules—I see no reason not to start at the top. Everybody tells me that means Daniel Baker, M.D., whose worshipful clients include Sophia Loren, Lauren Bacall, Nan Kempner, and Christopher Walken. When I call his office, though, I am told that there is a very long waiting list; the first opening for a consultation is thirteen months away. (I don't mention that I work for *Vogue*.) It sometimes seems as if the most expensive things in life have the longest waiting lists—six months for my Chanel suit and four years for my black leather Kelly bag. I soon find out just how expensive facial surgery can be. If a woman's face is her fortune, it now *costs* a fortune—$20,000 and up, depending on how much gets lifted. That evening, when I tell my husband that I booked my first consultation for a year from next month, he seems relieved. Anything can happen in a year, he reasons, including my coming to my senses.

The friendly secretary at the office of Sherrell Aston,

M.D., on the other hand, says she'll fit me into his busy schedule because she knows how "anxious" I must be, and she gives me an appointment five weeks down the road. Dr. Aston, who worked on Pamela Harriman, is a great favorite with the old-money crowd, and when I meet him in his Park Avenue office, I can see why. He's beautifully dressed in a well-cut dark suit and what must be a Sulka tie. He's just about the same height as my cousin Varaztad, and he pats my hand, gently and reassuringly, throughout the fifteen-minute consultation. He asks me what bothers me about my face. I tell him I don't like my worry lines and my smile lines, and I don't like being told I look tired. After studying my face from several different angles under a punishingly strong light, he gives my hand an extra-long squeeze and says, in his ever-so-slightly Southern accent, "I can make you better."

He proposes to do this with a face-lift and a brow-lift. The works. My stomach flip-flops. I'd been anticipating something less drastic. He hands me a mirror, pulls up the skin on my left cheek, and shows how the face-lift would minimize the smile lines but without getting rid of them completely. Then he shows how raising my eyebrows would smooth away the worry lines. "You don't have a problem with your eyes," he says. "The brow-lift would take care of any problem with the upper lids." My lower lids are fine, except for "a little scaling at the corner," which he could remedy with a laser. Nothing to it, except for the two- to three-week recovery period after surgery, and the fees, which I am to discuss with one of his many assistants after the consultation. (The total, including anesthesia and an overnight stay in the hospital, but without lasering, comes to $21,550, plus $150 for this initial visit.) We don't talk about the bad parts—the painful recovery period, the swelling and the black eyes, the rubber drains behind the ears for oozing blood, the trying to sleep in a sitting-up position to keep the stitches from pulling out, all of which I've read about, again and again. I do tell him that I'm terrified of needles, a real phobia. "Mark on her orange card that she gets no needles," he tells the nurse, without skipping a beat. "Gas and some pills, but no needles." And he gives my hand another deeply reassuring squeeze.

Brooke Astor likes to tell people that she's ninety-seven years old and has never had a face job. When Gloria Steinem turned fifty, she said proudly, "This is what fifty looks like." My sixty-two-year-old friend Brooke Hayward bristles at the very thought of cosmetic surgery. "I find it totally repellent," she says. "It's taken a lifetime to get the way I look. Of course, if I were ugly or disfigured, I might feel different." John Guare once told me that if his wife, Adele Chatfield-Taylor, ever got a face job, he'd punch her in the nose. No chance of that: Adele says she's "relieved to be my age. Wrinkles. Big deal." "All it really takes," John quips, "is Scotch Tape and rubber bands and a nail driven through the back of the head."

In spite of some similar feelings on my part, not to mention the strenuous resistance of my husband, I go to see Paul S. Striker, M.D., another Park Avenue wonder-worker, whose specialties, judging from the pamphlets on display in his waiting room, are "laser eyelid surgery" and "the new liposuction." He looks like a young Bob Dole, and he's as short as I am. (What is it about plastic surgeons and height?) The first thing he tells me, after the usual preliminary questions about why I've come to see him, is that my eyes are the real problem—just the opposite of what Dr. Aston said. "It's your eyes, definitely. Your upper eyelids are folding down, draping, festooning, bringing your eyes lower on your face. They're crashing right into your nose." Yikes! He lifts my brow with his hands. "You don't need a brow-lift," he says. "It wouldn't be right for you. You'd look like you were perpetually surprised. And you don't need a face-lift. There's nothing to lift. There's no fat." He brings out a stack of photographs, before and after headshots of patients. As we leaf through them, it occurs to me how I would hate to have my face in that stack. He talks about curing my worry and smile lines with injections of collagen, or better still, a little fat from my thighs. A fat injection lasts about a year, he says, collagen about three months or less. The eye surgery he has in mind would be done entirely by laser, which he switched to four years ago after two decades of cutting and suturing, because it's quicker, there's less bleeding, and the recovery time is shorter. The laser surgery is good for ten to fifteen years, he says, unless I cry a lot. "I had one patient who had laser eye surgery and then went through a horrible divorce. And after six months of crying, it was ruined. It also depends on your skin. You have to keep out of the sun and wear sunscreen." Although there's no fat to remove under my eyes, he says, he'd like to do a little laser resurfacing there. Assuming that I plan to go along with all this, he gives me endlessly complicated instructions about skin care and the proper use of Renova, a prescription creme with the miracle ingredient Retin A, which, as I later learn, helps to prevent the blotching that laser surgery can cause.

When I tell him I like the idea of borrowing fat from my thighs because I've always wanted to lose it there, he says, "Show me." I rise from the dentist-like examining chair and stand in front of him. "No," he commands, "let me see them."

Acutely embarrassed, I partially drop my pants. He studies me from every angle. "Liposuction will help you there. That's not going to go away, no matter how much you exercise or diet. That's there for good. Even if you were starving to death on a desert island, and you were skeletal everywhere else, that wouldn't go. You'd die before you'd lose it." That's just dandy, isn't it? And not even a hand squeeze to soften the blow. "But you don't need a face job. I wouldn't do a face job on you."

Lunch at Vivolo's with my friend Roxana. She knows seven women who have just had cosmetic eye surgery. Ten years ago, even five years ago, those women wouldn't have told her about it. Face jobs are out of the closet now, though; no more phony trips to Brazil to cover the post-op period of seclusion. Nearly three-and-a-half million Americans (both men and women) had their faces or bodies sculpted, rearranged, or re-created last year. And they seem to be doing it at younger and younger ages. Gerald Imber, M.D., author of *The Youth Corridor*, argues that the best approach is to nip aging in the bud with small cosmetic procedures from the age of thirty on up through the mid-fifties.

As it happens, Dr. Imber is next on my list. "Great name," he tells me, looking up from my chart. "Are you any relation to—" Yes, I am. Tieless and jacketless, hair slicked back like a tango dancer's, Dr. Imber exudes boundless confidence and authority. He's the only doctor who asks me, when I tell him that people say I look tired, "Well, are you tired?"

"As a matter of fact, yes."

"There you are. I can see exactly what you should do, and it will make an enormous difference." What he sees for me is a blepharoplasty for the upper eyelids, to cut away the excess fat and drooping skin, and one for under the eyes as well, to get rid of the fatty "bags" and the discoloration he finds there. Surprise. The other two doctors saw no fat under my eyes. He'll also cut the corrugator muscles, which go into action whenever you frown—I guess this means I won't be able to frown anymore. And he'll suction fat from my cheeks and inject it right into my smile lines and my worry lines. "It won't take the lines away totally, but it will make them look like they're just beginning." The fat injections, he says, would have to be repeated every six months. Dr. Striker said that they would last a year.

"So," I say nervously, "what are my options?"

"There are no options." Dazzling smile. "You have to do this."

"What about laser for the eyes?"

"No. That's no good for you, because you have Mediterranean skin, and laser treatment might make the skin under your eyes a different color from the rest of your face. And I don't recommend a face-lift for you. You have no wrinkles. You don't need that. You will—that's coming someday. But, right now, there're not enough lines or wrinkles to make it worthwhile."

I'm plenty confused by this time, and I get a lot more confused when I visit the next two surgeons on my list, Michael Kane, M.D., and Alan Matarasso, M.D. Both of them say that I need a face-lift *and* a brow-lift. What's happened, according to them, is that my eyebrows have dropped significantly. "Do you see how low your eyebrows are?" Dr. Matarasso asks me, as I gaze once again into a hand-held mirror. "They should be sitting right above the bone, but now they're below the bone." Instead of operating on the eyes, both Dr. Matarasso and Dr. Kane would prefer to do what Dr. Sherrell Aston recommended: an endoscopic brow-lift, which involves much less cutting than the old coronal brow-lifts and which shortens the forehead instead of making it higher. "Glenn Close has a very high forehead, and it makes her look older," Dr. Matarasso says. "She had a coronal brow lift, which pushed her hairline back even farther." But do I really want a shorter forehead? "Oh, yes," he says. "It's much more attractive." Well, okay, except I've always thought that the women with high foreheads look intelligent, and the ones with low foreheads look like stoats.

I ask Dr. Kane, the youngest of the doctors I talk to, whether there is any benefit to be gained from the new anti-aging cremes on the market. "Face creams are really a scam," he says. "They don't do it, and exercise doesn't do it." As a possible alternative to the brow job that he recommends for me, he tells me that he can inject my frown lines with Botox, which temporarily paralyzes the nerves around the corrugator muscles. Botox is derived from botulinum toxin, a deadly poison. I'll pass on that, thank you. And besides, it's hideously expensive: $650 a shot, repeatable in six months or earlier. Like Dr. Matarasso, though, he thinks my best course is a face-lift and a brow-lift, and he offers a special soup-to-nuts price, hospital and anesthesia included, of just under $17,000. (Dr. Matarasso's fee for approximately the same procedures comes to $24,000.) When I ask Dr. Kane how long his face job will last, he says, "Gravity is always at work, even from the day after you have the surgery. So maybe it'll last the traditional seven years, maybe eight, or maybe you'll never need it again. A lot has to do with your genes." The mention of gravity makes me think of Tallulah Bankhead's line, "When you're old, you have everything you had, except it's closer to the ground."

I have one more doctor on my New York plastic-surgeon-shopping spree (two, including the year-away Dr. Dan Baker), but before that, I have to go to Miami and to Los Angeles, so I decide to check out ace plastic surgeons in those image-conscious towns. The name Stephan Baker, M.D., comes up on my radar screen for Miami. He's young, tall (for a change), blond, and German-born, and he spends the first forty-five minutes talking about my ancestor, Dr. Kazanjian, and showing me book after book with pictures and articles about him. "This is the real thing," he says. "Reconstructive surgery for war victims. We don't get to see things like this anymore. We only get cosmetic things. Every once in a while we get an automobile accident victim or a baby with a cleft palate, but the other stuff . . ." The other stuff, in my case, seems to be the endoscopic brow-lift, and maybe a face-lift to make me feel refreshed. Another option, he says, would be Botox injections, but for those he says I should go to a dermatologist. "I'm going to tell you something controversial. Dermatologists are trying to do surgery, and plastic surgeons are trying to do dermatology. It's a turf war." If I decide on surgery with Dr. Baker—brow-lift, upper eyelids, face- and neck-lift—I can have it right away for the astonishingly low (!) all-inclusive fee of just over $10,000.

The main thing I learn from Frank Kamer, M.D., the veteran Los Angeles practitioner who has performed miracles for many of Hollywood's ageless charmers, is that I have great earlobes. What's good about them is that they're long and free-swinging, i.e., not connected to my cheeks, which makes them very useful for hiding the stitches from the full-dress face-lift he recommends for me. Somehow, this doesn't feel like a compliment, but at this point, I'm grateful for any positive signals. Kamer does not do laser or collagen or fat injections (he turns those over to the dermatologist who shares his office space; no turf war here), and he doesn't believe in implants for smile or worry lines. "They can float around," he says, "and get misplaced." In addition to a face-lift, he suggests getting rid of the fat under my eyes (the elusive fat that three other doctors have told me I don't have) and doing a coronal (high-forehead) brow-lift. "Accept the fact of a higher forehead," he advises. He also tells me that it's by no means too early to embark on cosmetic surgery. "You're entering the golden age, the years from forty-five to fifty-five." On my way out of the office, Kamer's "patient coordinator" tells me that the work will cost just under $30,000, but that (hooray!) I can pay for it with my American Express card. The frequent flyer miles I earn that way will let me travel business class to the hospital.

Back in New York, I go to see Craig Foster, M.D., who is a little over six feet tall and, I would guess, about my age. In spite of his towering reputation (he's the one who rebuilt the face of the Central Park jogger), he makes me feel comfortable and calm. He tells me, after a fairly brief examination, that I don't need a face-lift. "A face-lift doesn't do much for smile lines," he says. "It's more about sagging chins and jowls." He doesn't recommend a brow-lift either, and he doesn't think I should have eyelid surgery. "It's not going to make that much difference. If the lines bother you, I'd recommend collagen, provided you're not allergic to it."

Is collagen better than fat? I ask. (The three receptionists in his outer office had been talking about their collagen lip jobs.) Injecting fat is a surgical procedure, Dr. Foster says. "It's a big needle, and you can't inject it just under the skin; you have to go deeper. It works about eighty percent of the time, but in some cases you have to do it several times before it takes."

He comes up close and studies my face from both sides. "Listen," he says, gently, "if you were my sister, I'd tell you to go home. You don't need any face surgery."

So where am I? I've seen eight of the top cosmetic surgeons, and there's no clear consensus. I've been told I need a face-lift and a brow-lift. I've been told I don't need either—the problems can be solved by eyelid surgery (one would operate by laser, others by scalpel). Some doctors saw fat under my eyes, requiring lower lid surgery; others saw no fat. I've heard about fat injections, Botox injections, and collagen injections for my smile and worry lines. And I've been told it's too early for me to think about any of this. At no time did I feel that anyone was trying to sell me a bill of goods, or pushing one of the trendy new looks, like the narrow-tipped Michelle Pfeiffer nose. They all listened to what I wanted, and they all (with one exception) laid out the options and said the decision was up to me. The fact remains, however, that each doctor saw me differently. The surprising lack of consensus made me understand why this sort of plastic surgery is now being called "aesthetic" surgery. It's more an art than a science. Pending my still comfortably in-the-future appointment with Dr. Daniel Baker, I have to decide whether I really want to be raw material for this particular art form. Brooke Astor or Sophia Loren? To frown or not to frown? The decision, I guess, is already made.

I saw pale kings, and princes too,
   Pale warriors, death-pale were they all;
They cry'd—"La belle Dame sans Merci
   Hath thee in thrall!"

—JOHN KEATS, "LA BELLE DAME SANS MERCI"

The idea of the femme fatale has fascinated men for centuries, and for some reason it's always fascinated me. Pandora, Cleopatra, Lucrezia Borgia, Carmen, Lola Montes, Mata Hari, Sharon Stone, Jessica Rabbit, and all the other avatars of John Keats's belle dame sans merci fill me with wonder and curiosity, maybe because I'm so far from being a dangerous woman myself. How do they do it? How do they make men go clunk, throw away their crowns and empires, ditch their wives, commit suicide, and otherwise act like total idiots? Of course, some people will tell you that men don't need much prompting to act like that, and that the whole notion of the femme fatale is a male fantasy, an expression of their deepseated terror of female sexuality. Other people insist that whether or not such women existed in the past, they don't anymore—women now have too many other ways of getting and asserting power. I disagree. I think the idea is as firmly fixed today in the human psyche (both male and female) as it was when Homer sang of Odysseus and the Sirens. Look at the renewed spate of film-noir heroines like Kathleen Turner in *Body Heat,* Linda Fiorentino in *The Last Seduction,* and Sharon Stone in *Basic Instinct,* in which a female demon un-mans all the men in sight. Besides which, I know a few femmes who are pretty fatale, and if you think about it, you probably do too.

The fatal woman exists in many different forms and degrees, but let's be clear about who she is and isn't. In the movies, for example, Marlene Dietrich was often a femme fatale, and so were Greta Garbo, Louise Brooks, Barbara Stanwyck, Ava Gardner, and Jeanne Moreau; Mae West, Jayne Mansfield, Sophia Loren, Marilyn Monroe, and other world-class seductresses were not—they were insufficiently dangerous. The late Pamela Digby Churchill Hayward Harriman was the most successful courtesan of our era. She devoted expert attention and nurturing to a long line of grateful husbands and lovers, but she was never a femme fatale. Being a courtesan is a profession; being a femme fatale is a calling. A femme fatale is not in it for money or prestige or titles or love and marriage. She plays the game for its own sake, and in her case, the game means adventure, excitement, raw power, conquest. Often, but not invariably, she is very bad news for the men involved. Think of the male praying mantis, who literally loses his head to the conquering female. Think, for that matter, of the duke of Windsor. The woman is *fatal*, after all, and her intentions aren't honorable. She doesn't have to be beautiful. She doesn't have to be well dressed—or undressed. She doesn't even have to be young. All she has to be is irresistible, and I'd love to know how that's done.

Nobody wants to own up to being a femme fatale today, in this era of political correctness and feminist moralizing, and some leading feminists won't even discuss the subject. When Gloria Steinem's assistant heard that I wanted to interview her boss for this piece, her answer was "definitely not." Susan Faludi, who did talk to me about it, said that the femme fatale concept "says more about men's fear than it does about women's power. It's not surprising that the idea is coming back now, because it fits in beautifully with a victim culture, in that if something bad happens to me, it must be somebody else's fault. And a lot of bad things are happening to men these days. But what real woman ever was a femme fatale? I would be hard put to name one, although I can think of plenty in films."

I seem to keep hearing, though, about dangerous women in high places. The late Clare Boothe Luce "could slay any man she came across," says her biographer, Sylvia Jukes Morris. "It was like being dynamited by angel cake. I think she really set out to punish men because she felt her father had abandoned her." The artist Louise Bourgeois, whose highly erotic sculptures are in most of the leading museums, "has laid traps for men all her life," according to Museum of Modern Art curator Robert Storr. "Hers is a femme fatalism of the brain. A real femme fatale has to have a past. Louise has left a wake, and many people have been swept up in it."

Tania Bryer, the thirty-something British TV star, is already a retired femme fatale. Before her marriage to Tim Moufarrige, a celebrity sports agent, she was compared to Zuleika Dobson, the female juggernaut in Max Beerbohm's novel, for whom the entire male student body at Oxford drowns itself. "Knowing that other people are suffering because of you is a very odd feeling," Tania told me recently. "It's very strange. Sometimes you just want to block it out." But after each of her conquests—an Italian count, an Australian press baron, a Belgian banker—she tended to lose interest. "Once the challenge was up, that was it. My big important ones, the big three, they're still not married, which is interesting."

And then there's Wendy. Wendy lives in my building for part of the year, and even today, in her early fifties, she turns men goofy. "If she'd ever looked at my husband, I would have taken him to the Antarctic," a novelist friend of mine told me. "One day, years ago, I was walking on the street with a man, and we saw Wendy and her then-husband. Wendy was wearing tight jeans, curly black shoulder-length hair, big hat, sunglasses, long legs, and a great body. Instead of saying hello or shaking hands, she walked straight into the man I was with, stretching herself against him and wrapping her arms around him. It was a charming, irritating, hilarious, wonderful, sexual gesture. Wendy would look directly into a man's eyes, gaze into his soul. Any of us can gaze, but we have a tacit agreement that this is a weapon we don't use. She had a willingness to disengage from the rules of conduct."

Wendy is the genuine article. She's broken up countless marriages ("May I say on my behalf, three men who divorced their wives remarried them"), and any number of friendships between men. She tells me the number of men she's had and then forbids me to reveal it.

"You kept count?"

"My shrink once made me count." The numbers are a little hard to credit, considering that it easily outdistances Casanova's lifetime total of 123 women (including nuns), but I've checked with several alpha males and I'm inclined to believe everything Wendy says—almost. "I was always the aggressor," she goes on. "I've only been seduced once in my life, by a seventeen-year-old boy who was a virgin."

Among the men who have gone clunk over her, according to Wendy, are three movie stars (Warren Beatty, Steve McQueen, and Clint Eastwood), a network news anchor, an NFL football star, a *New York Times* correspondent, a legendary Knopf editor, three famous novelists, and "a big Mafia lawyer I met while I was on jury duty." She's also been married three times—her current husband is a Palestinian financier—and she has three grown daughters, two natural and one adopted. For a couple of years after the breakup of her first marriage, she supported herself and her kids by driving a New York City taxicab. "I was making $350, $400 a week. I got the best tips in the garage, and I didn't go to bed with any of my fares."

Needless to say, Wendy has ambivalent feelings about her erotic career. She's an intelligent, funny, self-aware woman, who knows perfectly well that her behavior isn't exactly normal. "How ghastly for somebody to be so insecure that she has to sleep with so many men," she confides at one point. "It was the hit, the hit, the hit. I never started anything thinking it would be a brief fling. Each time it was that this could be the biggest, most exciting, most passionate relationship that ever happened."

She attributes most of her insecurities to a pair of wildly promiscuous and narcissistic parents. Her father was a world-famous musician and performer whose instrument happened to be the harmonica. (Yes, the harmonica.) Wendy and her brother and sister grew up in a show-biz household, first in Los Angeles and then, when her father was blacklisted during the McCarthy period, in London. "I never had any love from my parents," she says, "but I had six years of love from my nanny, who on her day off took me with her. So I knew what love was." She fell in love for the first time at the age of eight, with a boy in her class at a Surrey boarding school. "We were caught in our pajamas, in bed, holding each other, with our little bottles of milk. We both were thrown out of school. I was just nuts about him." At the age of twelve, sitting in back of a car with a thirty-eight-year-old man whose wife was in the front seat with Wendy's mother, she let her hand fall next to his on the seat and felt a major rush when he began caressing it. "That I could get this older man interested in me—it was just thrilling. From then on, I went after anybody I wanted.

"What attracted me to married men was that I found them the easiest. You would see the very best of them, and it would have intrigue and danger, which spiced up everything. You were something they lived for and thought about all the time, and you were forbidden. What I would find is that I could turn myself into whatever their fantasy happened to be. I wanted to be irresistible because I found myself repellent. I never thought I was pretty. Even if I was thin and wore clothes well, I didn't have a good body. I thought I was stupid. My education had stopped pretty early [she married when she was sixteen].

I couldn't really do anything, but I could be the sexiest, most exciting woman."

All right, but how? What do you do? Is it something a girl like me could learn?

"The main trick—and it's not a trick for me because it's inherent—is absolute rabid curiosity about what makes this man tick," Wendy says. "He's never had such incredible, intense attention as he's getting from me. Eye contact is crucial, but not batting your eyes or obvious stuff like that. With me, part of it was just mischief. I wanted to make so much trouble. And it had to be fun."

One man who has known Wendy for twenty years without going to bed with her told me that she had a sort of "electricity" that was unique. It was partly her boldness, he said, her being able to say the most provocative and intimate things, and goading you to do the same. Others have mentioned that in spite of her obvious availability, there was always something unattainable about her. Clearly, just focusing your attention on the man is not enough—I do that all the time, when I'm interviewing people, and men don't fall like cordwood. (Come to think of it, though, I met my husband when I went to interview him for an article.) Sally Quinn, who has occasionally been tagged as a femme fatale, told me that all it takes is announcing to a man that you find him attractive. "Any woman who puts the burn on a guy is going to take him in," she said. "It doesn't require a lot of talent."

Are men really that dense? I suspect that flattery alone won't do it, either—something else is needed. It could be what the writer Francine du Plessix Gray refers to as "a kind of magnetic exhalation." Peter Foges, an independent television producer who says he knows a few femmes fatales around New York, speaks of their "strange kind of coquettish failure to consummate relationships, which can drive men quite mad with desire. To be a femme fatale is to imply that you're not conquerable. She's never yours. When you're with her, she may make you feel like you're the only one, but the next day you'll see her on the arm of another man. There's always something held back. The femme fatale is all about veils and disguise and not revealing everything, ever. If you look carefully at the Mona Lisa, you'll see that the two sides of her face are different—they're saying different things. This is why she's so very strange and alluring."

Michel Feher, a Paris-based philosopher who has spent some time researching the history of the femme fatale, sees it as "a figment of the male imagination" and a chapter in the history of misogyny. This "exciting fear or fearsome excitement," he argues, became a prominent literary construct in the nineteenth century as "a defense mechanism for frightened men who looked with horror on the prospect of female liberty and equality of the sexes." Feher identifies four types of femmes fatales, each of which can be seen to best advantage in films: (1) women who break the bonds between men (Garbo in *Flesh and the Devil* or Jeanne Moreau in *Jules et Jim*); (2) women who break up marriages (Marlene Dietrich in *The Blue Angel*); (3) women who make society crumble (Louise Brooks in *Lulu*); and (4) cold schemers who crave power and use men to get it (Barbara Stanwyck in *Double Indemnity*). "But are there femmes fatales *really*?" Feher asks. "Or is there a little femme fatale within every woman? The femme fatale is rooted in a very old-fashioned form of bourgeois misogyny, and thirty or forty years of feminism have changed that a bit. It seems that slowly but surely, women are constructing their own models of erotic life and erotic style."

But isn't it possible that the femme fatale can be a male fantasy and also a fact? And what about female fantasy and the homme fatal? Mario Praz, in his classic study *The Romantic Agony*, showed how French and English literature and society in the first half of the nineteenth century were permeated by the idea of the Byronic hero—the man who was "mad, bad, and dangerous to know." ("My embrace was fatal," declaims the protagonist of Byron's *Manfred*. ". . . I loved her, and destroyed her!") There may even be more fatal men than fatal women around today, although feminism and gay liberation tend to make that idea seem comical. Isaac Mizrahi, who jokes that he's always wished he could be seen as "a sort of fag fatal," proposes Matt Nye, "the one who captured Mr. *Rolling Stone*, Jann Wenner," as an up-to-date homme fatal. "It's the romance of the century," he said. "Like Wallis and Edward."

Whatever the secret is, I realize now that being a femme fatale is something that can't be learned. It's a charismatic power, and you're either born with it or you're not. It's not for sale—you can't buy it. It has nothing to do with clothes, or perfume, or plastic surgery, or wanting to get ahead, or even with sexual expertise. Madame Récamier, whose mysterious allure tormented Benjamin Constant and nearly drove the future king of Sweden to suicide, was widely believed to have remained a virgin. I find it sort of wonderful and scary to think that these fabulous creatures are still loose in the world, rogue flames surrounded by doomed male moths, carrying out their mysterious work. Wendy says she now regrets all the marriages she broke up, but she's not ashamed of being a femme fatale. "And I still think that I'm a nice person," she tells me. "I think I have a good heart. I never went after anyone who belonged to a woman friend of mine. I'd never go after your husband, for example—unless, of course, you offered him to me as a present."

The Ball Gown

It's been a long time since I bought a ball gown. Sardella of

Newport (Rhode Island) did my coming-out dress—a simple

white sheath whose bodice was smothered in handmade flow-

ers made of the same antique satin—and that was it for the

next twenty-five years. Somehow, although I live in Manhattan and go out a fair amount, I've never felt the need for another Really Big Evening Dress. In the last year, however, one of my oldest friends celebrated a major wedding anniversary with a dinner dance at the Marble House in Newport, and my husband and I got invited to a white-tie evening at the Whitney Museum, and at both of these affairs, I found myself feeling a little Bo-Peepish in my old Sardella, which I resurrected from its quarter-century sleep. I've also started to feel slightly drab in the five-year-old Comme des Garçons black evening suit that I usually wear to any and every black-tie event. My friend Eric says black makes me look like a Sicilian widow.

Women, it seems, are dressing up more at night. The fashion press at the moment is up to its hips in opulent new party gowns. Whatever the reasons—millennial expectations, a surfeit of minimalism, the rebirth of glamour—a lot of us apparently have the urge for clothes that will make us feel not just good but glorious. I certainly do. I want to be ready for the next big-time invitation, and I want to be noticed in a new way. Ah, but a girl's reach should exceed her grasp, or what's a ball gown for? My fashion-savvy friend Dana, who may have been talking to Eric, tells me to look for something beaded and pastel. "No black," she says. "Branch out." With that in mind I enlist Dana to case the uptown designer boutiques with me on the last Monday in December.

We start with Givenchy on Madison Avenue. I've never been in Givenchy before, and I'm a little scared. Givenchy and Audrey Hepburn are twinned in my mind, way up there on Fashion Olympus. And Alexander McQueen, the house's current designer, is fashion's bad boy—his spring collection features the Dolly Parton look, with tight white leather and fringe. Dana gives me courage, though; her tall, blond, confident good looks make me less self-conscious about being short and dark. The store is actually quite inviting, and Peggy, the saleswoman who helps me, seems friendly. Their spring line isn't in yet, and when I ask to see a book of the spring collection, Peggy's candor surprises me. "Oh, we never bother with that. Alexander McQueen uses the shows to get publicity. It's his art, you know." She rolls her eyes. "Those clothes are never even made, let alone sold here."

At Prada, austerity rules. Very few clothes, presented like paintings on museum walls; immaculate vitrines for wisps of underwear; curatorial salespersons who pay me no attention. I look at some filmy organza tops—totally see-through—with beaded hemlines and matching see-through skirts. Not for me, thanks. On to Dolce & Gabbana, where we see, set up in one of the Madison Avenue windows, a banquet table with candelabras, majolica, and so much food that it looks like a still life of an orgy. What's the message? Forswear this if you want to wear our clothes? I go to the back of the store and find a salesgirl named Sonia sitting at a table. She permits me to try on a long white chiffon coatdress with huge red poppies. Nope. I feel short and plump and exposed. While I'm changing, she goes to the basement and comes back with spring gown accessories—a tiny, bright blue mink bolero and the smallest flesh-colored mink stole with tulle sleeves attached. I try on the bolero, and it looks fabulous (it should, at $3,350). Sonia is trying on the stole. She's forgotten me. I ask if she'd mind letting me try it on, and, somewhat reluctantly, she does. Adorable, expensive ($2,985). Now all I need is the dress.

At the Versace boutique on Madison, Dana helps me into a red silk number that lays me bare on one side from neck to midcalf. This isn't how I want to be noticed. The only other spring dresses here are black, with red or aqua lining, so we don't tarry. Walking down Madison, I see two long dresses in the window of La Perla. Does La Perla do evening dresses, in addition to bathing suits and underwear? We go in and ask a salesgirl, who says, "Yes, we do *outerwear*." I try on a flesh-colored piece of outerwear in a sparkly fabric. Unlike every other dress I've seen, it hugs and supports my bodice the way

La Perla underwear does, and it looks and feels great on me. Better still, it costs only $964. I could spring for this. But there are miles to go before I make my decision.

At Valentino, we see exquisite beaded gowns, and I'm appalled to see that they're $11,000 and up. I know someone who borrows dresses like this from Chanel whenever she needs to because she won't be seen in the same dress twice; I don't have that sort of clout, and I plan to wear my Big Evening Dress as often as I can. Across the street at Armani, we wander casually into what may be the fourth-floor VIP lounge—the door is open. By-invitation-only VIP lounges with all sorts of fancy appointments and services are the latest innovation in fashion boutiques, but when salesperson Michelle finds us non-VIPs, she is cordiality itself. She brings me a white silk crepe with a halter-like neck from their cruise line. It's beautifully cut, as all of Armani's clothes are, but it's a little dull, and too unforgiving for my body. Many of the new evening dresses reveal so much body that underwear is taboo. Michelle brings out the books for spring—flowing chiffons in navies and beiges, beading, breasts showing through, sexy simplicity, wonderful clothes if you happen to look like Gwyneth Paltrow.

At Barneys, where most of the designers have boutiques, I try Vera Wang's ice-blue matte-jersey gown, high-necked, with a slit up to my waist in front. "Boring," says Dana. Donna Karan's long matte-jersey skirt with a matching T-shirt is not boring, but it's also not Big Evening enough. There's more Dolce & Gabbana spring stuff here than there was at the D & G uptown boutique, but their long, fitted chiffons with big yellow lemons are for tall girls, and the patterns strike me as more suitable for tablecloths.

They have a few pastel chiffon gowns for spring at Calvin Klein, but nothing in my size, and besides, I'm not comfortable with this store's cool minimalism, and I'm a little tired of being ignored by haughty salespersons. It's two-thirty, time for lunch.

Forty-five minutes later we hit Bergdorf's fourth floor. Spring has not yet arrived for Oscar de la Renta. When I ask Rona, my saleslady, if she can show me anything by John Galliano, whose new boutique just opened two floors below, she looks stricken. Does she think I'm too old for Galliano? "You're more for this floor," she temporizes. Dana and I go to the Galliano boutique anyway. It's fantasyland—pink bows painted on the walls, zebra skin on the floor, a cloud painting overhead. Randy, an intensely serious-looking salesman, helps me pick out a couple of dresses—a pale bordeaux organza over a silk slip of the same color ($4,060), with "the best spaghetti straps I've ever seen," according to Dana, who had spaghetti for lunch; and a long gray-blue slip dress, also organza over silk, with the same delicious straps ($1,705). The bordeaux Galliano doesn't even have a zipper, but I wriggle into it. "This is interesting," Dana says. I like the sense of playfulness about the dress. It really fits me, and even without a bra I don't feel too exposed. The gray-blue is just as good on me. These dresses are flowing, sexy, pretty, and youthful, with a whimsical quality. For the first time, I'm starting to feel hopeful.

Galliano also designs for Dior, but Bergdorf Goodman doesn't carry Dior, so we go to the Dior shop a few blocks down Fifth Avenue. The first thing we see is a large-screen video of the spring collection. It's mesmerizing, different from any fashion show I've ever seen, a piece of theater; instead of marching back and forth on a runway, the models lounge on an antique bed, circle a billiard table, and move about in what looks like the private chambers of a seventeenth-century châ- teau. They wear fantastic headpieces, marabou scarves and pocketbooks, elaborate jewelry. Their dresses are beaded and meshed and fringed, dashingly cut away and slashed to show succulent *tranches* of leg and torso, a medley of dusty colors and slithering fabrics in which the difference between innerwear and outerwear gets lost. I'm totally seduced, and so is Dana. We go up the winding staircase and wait for the one visible saleswoman to finish a long telephone conversation. She has only one dress for me to try. It's not like the ultra-romantic costumes on the video (which start at $15,000), but it's alluring—long, white, and splashed with navy blue daisies, with navy spaghetti straps and trim, and believe it or not, the price is a mere $1,820. It fits me perfectly and reminds me of an old Dior bathing suit I had years ago, which I wore until it fell apart one day in the pool at the Watergate, where I used to live. It was simple and flattering. But simple and flattering isn't quite what I have in mind for my ball gown.

We pass up Gucci, where I've heard that the new look for spring evenings is a rhinestone-studded bikini under sheerest chiffon, and decide to brave the latest Versace palazzo, on Fifth Avenue. There's a potentially interesting apricot beaded chiffon gown that I didn't see at the Madison Avenue boutique. As I reach to touch the material, a brusque salesgirl pushes my hand away, snarling, "Don't pull at it. I'll get it for you." No, thanks. If you're not a VIP, fashion boutiques can be rough going.

———————

Since Badgley Mischka designed Dana's wedding gown in 1990, they have become the reigning sovereigns of evening wear, with a clientele that includes Winona Ryder, Claudia Schiffer, and Blaine Trump. They've invented the modern ball gown—doing away with columns and full taffeta skirts and heavy construction, and cutting close to the rib cage. The day after our boutique marathon, Dana and I go to see them at their showroom on Seventh Avenue. James Mischka is tall, blond, and reticent. Mark Badgley is equally tall, dark, and outgoing.

They pull out some things they think would work for me, samples from their spring collection. Turning to James, Mark says, "She'd be great in the Nervous Flower Dress." Their dresses all have names; the Nervous Flower Dress's real name is Nicolette. It's pinky-gray, jewel-encrusted, and formfitting (but not see through), sleeveless, with a scoop neck, clusters of "nervous flowers" (peony-colored crystals) on both shoulders, and a fishtail train in back. The fit is incredible; it does unexpected things for my body and for my morale, but somehow, the nervous flowers are a little too much for me. Mark agrees. I try on Helena, Emily, Carly, and Karen, each of which (whom?) has a distinct personality, compacted of exquisitely layered European fabrics and the most intricate handwork (the beading is all done at Badgley Mischka's work-room in Bombay). Every one they show me ends in a fishtail. I envision mermaid women all over town, swishing their tails. "To be honest," Mark admits, "half our customers chop off the fishtail."

Next comes Roxana, an amber-colored georgette confec-tion entirely covered with rice pearls and faceted topaz crys-tals arranged to form little flowers. The dress looks both ultra-contemporary and antique. When I get into it, the feeling is indescribable. I've never worn a piece of clothing that has this kind of transforming magic. Where is my pumpkin coach? The color complements my skin and seems to light it up in a new way. Black never did this for me; branching out never felt so good. Roxana scoops me up, holds me in its firm but gentle $4,000 embrace, makes me forget that I'm only five foot two. "Thumbs-up," says Dana.

I take it off and put on Tallulah, which is made of what James calls clipped satin, lilac and green, touched up with sequins. Same body-friendly silhouette as Roxana but not as drop-dead good-looking as far as I'm concerned, and about a thousand dollars more expensive. "It's bias cut, so it really drops into the body," Mark says. Marcelle is next, at $4,460. "She's French," he says. It's pale bluish-beige, filmy and del-icate and elegant, with great little cap sleeves. I love myself in it. It's hard to decide. Marcelle seems more elegant, but I feel more glamorous in Roxana. Elegance or glamour? Is Marcelle more appropriate for my age than Roxana?

"Never ask that question," James says. "You should say, 'Is this dress the age I want to look?' "

Dana wants to see me in Roxana again. I put it on and get the same complex jolt of thrilling sensations. "This is a killer," Dana says. This is ridiculous. How can some stitched-together fabrics and beads make me feel like a Hollywood glamour queen? I know better, of course, and yet . . . If I get this dress, I'll never need plastic surgery or a shrink or another ball gown as long as I live.

Maybe that's how I'll justify it to my husband.

The Thighs

Here I go again. Three years have slipped by since my
all-out campaign to get rid of the fat thighs I've had since I
was a toddler, and just as everyone predicted, they've come
back. Lack of will power and too much New York stress have

undermined my resolve, and once more I feel uncomfortably tight in my jeans and embarrassed to be seen in a bathing suit. But why do I care? "I can see doing something about it if you're a twenty-year-old model," says my friend Brooke, "but what's the point at our age?" The painter Jennifer Bartlett says that forty-three is the last year a woman looks good—it's the transition between being an old young person and a young old person. That magic number is getting too close for comfort. I want to make one last run for the thighs of my dreams. And so I call up Ann Piccirillo, the exercise guru who miracle-whipped my legs into shape last time, and ask if she'll help me again.

"Okay," she says, a little dubiously, "but this is it." Ann runs Manhattan Body, the uptown exercise studio, and she doesn't really like to work with people individually. She also happens to be three months pregnant. We agree to work together for six months, in half-hour sessions three to five times a week. I'll take her body-toning classes whenever I can and go on the diet she prescribes. She'll be a mother at the end, and I'll be a sylph. Maybe.

At our first session, I discover that some things will be the same as the last time around, and others won't. Instead of having me ride the hated stationary bicycle for up to an hour a day, Ann is going to try a new technique she has invented—

precisely positioned weights for spot reducing. She straps two-pound weights to specific muscle groups on each thigh and has me exercise my legs in ways that work the quads, the hamstrings, the inner and the outer thighs, the buttocks, and the "saddlebag" area just south of the hips. She moves the weights around inside tourniquet-like rubber straps so that they press directly on each muscle. Ouch! It's such hard work that my overindulged thighs don't seem to think they can do it. Ann is pitiless. At the end of the first half hour, we've worked every leg muscle I have, and maybe some I don't, and I'm in considerable pain.

Now comes the bad news. My diet is going to be even more punitive than the last time. Ann wants me to give up bread completely, cut my pasta intake to two servings a week, and to do without potatoes, rice, bananas, grapes, carrots, egg yolks, and popcorn. No sweet desserts, needless to say. Basically a superlow-carbohydrate diet. And absolutely no bubbles—Diet Coke and other carbonated beverages are taboo. I was expecting the no-bread-and-no-bubbles regimen; both had been prohibited the last time. Ann had told me that the yeast in bread keeps on expanding inside the body, but she had never managed to explain to me why bubbles were bad. "I still can't get any doctor to agree with me," she says now, "so you're just going to have to take my word for it. Doctors do admit that bubbles cause bloating and distension, and I'll go on record saying they bloat your thighs. I've seen it with my own body, and I've seen it with so many of the bodies I've trained."

Unfortunately, spaghetti and Diet Coke are my staples. I have pasta for lunch and spaghetti for dinner most days, never with sauce, just a touch of extra virgin olive oil and a dusting of grated Parmesan. And I often choose a restaurant based on how good the bread is, more than the cuisine. Now I find myself subsisting mainly on salads, vegetables, fish, chicken, steak, and Wasa crackers. Hardly prison rations, but passing up pasta or sitting through a movie without popcorn and Diet Coke give me serious withdrawal symptoms. On the other hand, who said this was going to be easy?

At my next session with Ann, I confess that I had a roll with dinner last night—one of Da Silvano's irresistable little florets of manna. "Oh, no," she groans. "This is going to take a lot longer if you don't behave." She pulls out a red measuring tape, checks my waist and hips, and then zeros in on the trouble zone: right thigh, 21 inches; left thigh, 20½; right leg just above the knee, 16½; left leg, 16. "You've got an upper-leg problem. They're round and they don't have shape, the saddlebags are not so good, and your right leg is fatter than your left. But people are always too interested in how many inches they can take off. What's really important is the shape, and that's what I want to work on with you." I'd never thought about measuring my thighs. Can my right thigh really be as big as my waist? I went right home after the exercise session and measured my husband's thighs—20 inches each. Outrageous. My cat's left thigh is 5 inches. (She wouldn't let me get the other one.) An elephant's is 44 inches. Marilyn Monroe had 21-inch thighs, the same as mine, but she was three inches taller than I am, and the ideal body type then was more zaftig. Kate Moss's thighs, the thighs of the moment, are 18 inches thin.

During the next month, I find myself becoming more and more addicted to the exercise routines. Ann never has me do the same set of exercises twice. She's amazingly inventive about thinking up new ways to torture the same muscle. Every session is painful, but I'm making progress, so I don't mind. I find myself cheating less on the diet. After going away for a week and being what I thought was pretty conscientious about exercise and meals—no bread, no rice, no potatoes, no floating islands—I get a decidedly critical once-over from Ann at our next session. She grabs my outer thighs, kneading them like bread. "There's too much food in there," she says. "Are you drinking any bubbles?" When I fess up to one Diet Coke on the trip, she says, "Oh, well, that's what did it." I admit to drinking a bottle of San Pellegrino water a day and half a glass of red wine with dinner. "What? Well, stop that, too. And cut back to only one pasta a week. I don't like the way your legs are looking. They're not moving fast enough." We have decided to meet five times a week instead of three. She also wants me to drink at least eight glasses of purified still water a day—to flush out bad vibes, I suppose.

Ann keeps trying to find a medical authority who will back up her bubble theory. I try, too. I put in a call to Isadore Rosenfeld, M.D., whose new book, *Doctor, What Should I Eat?* (Random House), made the bestseller list. He says he'll get back to me. He does: "Listen," he says, "this is bullshit. Although I never like to argue with anybody's original research, I can find no reference to it in the scientific literature. And if I could, I'd be at a loss to explain it."

Now for something completely different. At a formal dinner party, I find myself sitting next to Leonard Lauder, grand pooh-bah of the world-conquering Estée Lauder cosmetics firm. When I pass up dessert, he asks me why. I tell him I'm on a thigh-reduction program that I'm writing about. "I can take two inches off your thighs with no exercise and no diet," he announces. Really? How? It seems that Estée Lauder is about to come out with a new cellulite product called

ThighZone Body Streamlining Complex, which they've been testing for two years. "This one really works," he insists. The next morning, two shapely, powder-blue bottles of ThighZone are delivered by messenger. Naturally, I am intrigued. Before using it, I go to see Estée Lauder's research scientists, who are a bit more cautious than Leonard. They don't guarantee that I'll lose inches. What ThighZone really does, they tell me, is restore elastin and collagen in the skin, making the skin tighter and firmer, and in the process doing a real number on the dreaded cellulite. "Women's skin is thinner than men's," one of them tells me. As he goes on to explain, female fat stacks up in columns, which poke through the skin to make the dimpled, icky look of cellulite. The fat in men's thighs accumulates in cross-hatched diagonals, and men's tougher, thicker skin helps to keep it in its place. "It just proves," he says, "that God is a man." There have been plenty of other cellulite-reducing cremes on the market lately, but they haven't worked too well. What's different about ThighZone is that it supposedly rebuilds the skin. (We'll see about that.) But you have to apply it morning and night for eight to sixteen weeks before you see any results, they say. I'll try it, Leonard, but I'm also going to do what Ann Piccirillo tells me.

At the end of my next session with Ann, she has me speed-walking around the room with four-pound weights bouncing and jouncing against my legs. She speed-walks right behind me, periodically grabbing my bottom to make sure I remember to keep a tight butt. It's like a bad dream. But things are happening. "The legs look good," she says, "but I think I can get another inch off." I take her class afterward, and I can't believe these are my legs in the mirror. I always felt that mine were the worst in the class, but now I'm almost proud of them.

SO IT MAY BE TRUE AFTER ALL: EATING PASTA MAKES YOU FAT

Believe it or not, this headline appears on the front page of the February 8, 1995, *New York Times*. They've discovered that people often gain weight on low-fat diets, and that simple carbohydrates—pasta, bread, and so forth—can encourage the production of body fat. I can hardly wait to hear what Ann has to say about this. "I've been saying it for years," she chortles. "You'll see. In the future they're going to discover about bubbles."

My legs have been shrinking ever since I went cold turkey on San Pellegrino, but there's no way to know whether it's the bubbles, the bread, the pasta, the exercise, or the ThighZone. My thighs are down to 19¼ inches and 19 inches, and my above-the-knees to 15½ inches. My hips are 33½ inches, just right, according to Ann. "When we started, I said I'd try to make your thighs look good. We're already there. Now I'm going to aim for excellent." She pulls the red tape extra-tight and says my thighs would be "perfection" at 19 inches on top and 14 inches below.

"Can you make me perfect?" I plead.

"Let's shoot for excellent. What are you trying to do to me? I'm six months pregnant." As I've been getting slimmer, Ann has been getting bigger, but not in the thigh area.

We're deep into the third month, and friends are telling me I look *too* thin. "Don't lose any more," warns Adele. "Lose twenty more pounds," says her ever-perverse husband, John. "You can be the invisible *Vogue* writer." Funny thing is, I haven't lost any weight on this diet. As a matter of fact, I've gained a pound. On an impulse, I take some new measurements at home and find I have lost an inch around the bust. Curses! Ann tells me I'm being too conscientious with my diet. "You won't even put milk on your cereal or eat the things you're allowed to eat," she scolds. "You have to eat some fat. I believe that fats go to the upper body, not the lower body. And besides, it's much easier to lose weight up there than down below." I'm ordered to go from skim to 1 percent milk and to indulge my love for Breyers Reduced Fat Swiss Almond Fudge Twirl ice cream. She also gives me arm exercises (military presses with six-pound weights) to develop my deltoids and upper body. Ann believes in sculpting the whole body. Wider shoulders make the hips and legs look narrower.

The next morning, Ann hands me a slip of paper with the name of someone who might be able to clear up the Great Bubble Mystery. I call Edythe Heus, who describes herself as a chiropractor who also does kinesiology (muscle therapy), "acupuncture diagnosis, a lot of Eastern stuff, homeopathic medicine, nutrition, cranial-sacral work, pretty much all body work, and also emotional remedies." Our conversation goes this way:

"Are bubbles bad for you?"

"Absolutely."

"Can you tell me why?"

"Bubbles impair digestion. Poorly digested foods have to be stored somewhere, and they're going to be stored in fat cells."

"Could that affect my thighs?"

"How tall are you?"

"Five-two."

"No wonder! Different body types assimilate food differently. When you're under five-three, weight gain usually sits in the saddlebag area." She explains in considerable depth about kidney function, calcium absorption, pH factors, and other arcane aspects of bubble trouble.

"So you go along with Ann's theory of no bubbles and no bread?"

"Absolutely."

We're coming to the end of the third month, and my cravings for something to substitute for the loss of bread, potatoes, and rice are going in some weird directions. One night, while feeding Penelope, my stepcat, I actually think her Iams smell pretty good.

Ann is so pleased with our progress that she has choreographed a new body-toning class based on her work with me and her invention, which she's decided to call Focus Weights. "Did you notice that your legs looked better than anybody's in the class?" she asks one day. "I was a little afraid to compare them, but thank God, they have great shape now." My husband has been saying the same thing for a couple of weeks. I'm down to 19-inch upper thighs and 14 inches above the knees—no Kate Moss, but perfection for me. My hips are 32½ inches, and my bust has sneaked back to where it was before. Ann has me on maintenance now. "The way I see it for you, for the rest of time you can have two glasses of red wine a week, and three bad carbos—maybe one rice, one potato, and one pasta."

"What about bread?"

"Have a piece of bread instead of one of the carbos and see what happens."

Maintenance also means spending fifteen minutes every day working with the leg weights at home. I take three body-toning classes a week—not so bad—and I've made a solemn vow to keep my saddlebags from filling up again. And no bubbles! Crazy as it sounds, I'm convinced, so convinced I don't even long for Diet Coke anymore. My secret hunch is that the spot-reducing exercises really worked, and Ann's diet nailed down the victory. As for ThighZone, I'm in my twelfth week now, and I'd say it's definitely smoothed and tightened my skin. I'll keep on using it. Why break up a winning combination?

Whether I can hold on to my new thighs is anybody's guess. I'm on my own now and cautiously optimistic. Call it the triumph of hope over experience.

The Fur Coat

It's hard to believe I'm doing this—shopping for a fur. I

grew up dreaming of being swathed in the softest and most

luxurious of furs (like the unforgetable chinchilla trenchcoat

that Greta Garbo wore in *Grand Hotel*), but I never was; and for the last ten years, cowed by the animal-rights activists and their sympathizers, one of the most ardent of whom was my stepdaughter, I've been perfectly content in my obviously fake spotted-cat coat. But that coat is coming apart at the seams. Besides which, my stepdaughter is going off to school in France for a semester; Naomi Campbell, who posed nude for animal activist ads ("I'd rather go naked than wear fur") is now wearing fur again; and recent issues of *Vogue* and *Harper's Bazaar* have been trumpeting the news that fur is not only acceptable, it's inescapable. Fur trim on suits and jackets, mink T-shirts, blazers in broadtail, sweaters with fur collars—everything seems to come with fur these days, and the hippest young designers are literally turning the fur coat inside out. So, anyway, here I am going off with my infuriatingly opinionated friend Belle to buy my first fur coat.

We start at Gucci, on Fifth Avenue at Fifty-fourth Street. The thermometer is in the 90s (it's early August in Manhattan), and I feel a little silly asking a saleswoman to lead me to the furs. "I'm interested in those short, bright colored ones I saw in the fashion magazines," I say.

"Oh, yes. The chubbies. Get ready." I follow her around the corner and there they are—bright yellow, ice blue, fire-engine red, and black, made of long-haired fox and taking up a lot of space. They're $9,000 each. "Isn't the blue beautiful?" she says. "Not the yellow—it makes you look like Big Bird."

"Why not yellow?" Belle demands. "Yellow is the most alive and the most advanced. The blue is dead-looking."

"Why not indeed," the ever-cheerful salesperson agrees. She unlocks it from its electronically alarmed umbilical cord, and I disappear into it. "That's marvelous," shouts Belle. "And you can really carry it," the saleswoman lies. I'm absolutely smothered in this ridiculously fluffy fox. It's meant to be a jacket, but it comes to my knees. An older blond woman across the way bursts out laughing. "Try on the red," Belle orders. I do—anything to get out of the yellow. "That's nice," Belle says, "but not as good. Try the blue." When I do, she proclaims it "hideous." To make matters worse, I can see that I don't have the legs for this. You need long thin legs to wear a chubby, and I don't have them. These furs aren't for me, no matter what Belle and the saleswoman may think, but Gucci doesn't have any other furs at the moment. Time to flee.

We walk two blocks up the avenue to Fendi, which is to fur what Hermès is to leather—the best of the best. Karl Lagerfeld designs their coats. I've been told to ask for Jack Cohen, which I do as soon as we get out of the glass elevator on the second floor. A man in a white vest detaches himself from several others and asks, "How did you hear about me?" I mumble something about a friend in Newport. "What would you like to look at?" asks Jack. I tell him I'm shopping for my first fur, probably my only fur. "Trust me," he says. "I know exactly what's right for you and I know exactly what size you are." Of course he does; we're exactly the same height.

He goes to a rack and comes back with a glossy, undyed mink coat. "Just try this on," he says. It's unlike anything I've ever worn and incredibly seductive. There's fur inside the pockets. It's unbelievably light in weight. "It's not lined, and it breathes," he says. "You can see right through it." He pulls the coat off me and holds it up to the light, which comes right through the exquisitely stitched seams. He turns the sleeves inside out and puts it on me with the fur against my skin. Now it's a milk-chocolaty suede coat with mink trim. Few things in life can feel this good. It's also very high-style, cut and shaped in all sorts of subtle ways that treat fur like fabric; it hugs the body and has its own mink belt. The bad news is that it costs $35,000. As I learn later, Fendi has two lower-priced lines—a medium-priced one, which is available at Saks, and the lower-priced Fendissimo—but Jack Cohen sells only the haute couture line.

"What else do you have?" Belle asks. Jack brings out a midcalf-length brown mink that's dotted with another kind of fur. He tells me the dots are made of something called "ory-lag," a Fendi-engineered cross between rabbit and chinchilla. This one is looser and more casual. Instead of a collar, it comes with a sort of mink ascot as an accessory. It reverses, too, but the inside is nylon so that it becomes a raincoat. My husband would approve—he's always bugging me to get a raincoat. While I'm thinking this, Jack is pulling a mink cap on my head, with an Elmer Fudd visor, and slinging a mink shoulder bag with a mink strap diagonally across my chest. He makes me walk to the big mirror up front, past a gaggle of salespeople who have been following every phase of Jack's performance and nodding approval at regular intervals. Belle loves this one, more than the yellow Big Bird job at Gucci. It costs $30,000, which is at least a small step in the right direction. (Coats don't get much lower than this at Fendi, where Russian sables run from $200,000 to $300,000, and chinchillas start at $75,000.)

"Wouldn't a longer coat make me look taller?" I ask Jack.

"Long is not for you. You're too short. Nothing is going to make you look taller."

"What about color, like a bright red or yellow?"

"Color is out."

"But I've just seen it in *Vogue*."

"Don't believe what you read in magazines."

"What about that one over there, the short gray one trimmed in chinchilla with the cinched waist?"

"That's cha-cha. That's glamour. And you're not glamour."

Thanks, Jack. I tell him I like the orylag dotted coat but that I have to bring my husband in to look at it. "Where is he? Can you call and get him in right now?"

"I'll bring him on Monday."

"We don't hold coats," Jack tells me as he removes my mink, "and this is the only one of these I have. I would advise you to bring your husband in as soon as possible."

Now I'm really hooked. When I started out, I wasn't absolutely sure I wanted a fur coat, but the Fendi experience changed that. People have been wearing fur for at least a hundred thousand years, I tell myself, and anyway, I've never been too correct politically: I eat lamb chops, I wear leather belts and shoes, I voted for Bush. But where am I? Nowhere. I want a fur coat that doesn't look like one of the behemoths my grandmothers used to wear, and I would like it to cost less than the country house I'm always hoping to find. Karl Lagerfeld changed the way we think about fur when he started designing for the Fendi sisters in the 1960s. More and more designers have followed his example in recent years; today more than 160 are designing fur fashions, compared with only forty-two in 1985. Marc Jacobs, Michael Kors, Narciso Rodriguez, and other cutting-edge talents have taken grandma's mink and sheared it, plucked it, slashed it, turned it into chesterfields, cardigans, ski vests, and short, zip-front warm-up jackets with hoods. Marc Jacobs shocked the industry by shearing sable, the holy of holies, more or less the most expensive fur in the world. There's a lot of sheared mink around, but from what I've seen, sheared mink looks like velvet, or even acrylic pile. You can dye it any color you want and make it look as fake as Dynel. What's the point? If I were a mink, to say nothing of a sable, I'd be very irritated. Being killed is bad enough without the dishonor of a short haircut. I don't want sheared mink, but I do want a modern look—a fur bridge to the next century.

The day after my shopping expedition with Belle, I stop in to see Isaac Mizrahi, who used a lot of recycled fur in his last collection. "What is more beautiful than fur?" he rhapsodizes. "Nothing. What is more horrible than fur? Nothing. I've thought it and thought it and thought it through, and I just come back to my original feeling, which is that fur is the greatest luxury known to man. You have to acknowledge the perversity of it. I mean, you acknowledge how perverse foie gras is, but a world without foie gras would be a terrible place." He also knows just what kind of fur would look right on me—a classic 1940s mink with a big shawl collar and huge cuffs, midcalf-length, like the one Bette Davis wore in *All About Eve.* "If you had one of those coats, baby, you'd just be so chic. Over a slip, over pants, over anything, over nothing." Is anybody doing coats like that today? "Me," he says, his mind obviously whirring. "I'm going to do that next fall."

But I can't wait. A lot of my friends have shearling coats from Searle, and to me they look neat, understated, and most of all, warm. The great thing about Searle is that you can choose a model from their designer collection and have it made to order in your size and in a variety of colors. I visit the Searle at Madison and Fifty-eighth, and what I like best are the two new ankle-length coats, at $3,700 each. They're beautiful, but they're very heavy, and they don't make me feel transcendent. (I've got to stop thinking Fendi.) I put on the long, navy blue wrap coat again. The saleswoman says that if I buy it now, I can still get a 10 percent discount from the sale that ended yesterday. "This coat is for you," she informs me. "You look wonderful in it, and I want you to have it."

I don't think about furs again until Monday. For some reason I drag my husband into Fendi, even though the prices make it pure fantasyland for me. Up the glass elevator to the second floor, where Jack Cohen is once again on the qui vive. He brings out the dotted mink orylag for me to try on (it's still

there), but then, instantly picking up on my husband's somewhat negative body language, he says, "Let me show you the
other one she was considering." He brings over the high-style
belted mink, holds it up to the light and flops it on the floor,
talks about transparency, and shows how it reverses to brown
suede. "These are all made by hand in Rome," he says. "If
you saw what goes on in the workroom, you'd want to pay
extra." More trips to the big mirror, with the attendant sales
crew nodding and smiling. Somehow we get out of the sales-
room without embarrassing ourselves. On the way down in the
elevator, my husband says he thought the orylag coat looked
like an animal with smallpox. He also confides that, even if
we could afford such a coat, it looks so *grande luxe* that he
would feel he had to walk three paces behind me on the street
when I wore it.

"The silhouette of the fur coat has changed pretty dra-
matically in the last couple of years," I am told by Jack Pearson, the former head of the Saks Fur Salon and also the former
fashion director of the Fur Information Council of America.
"We've gone from very full, swingy coats to a straighter silhouette. I attribute this mainly to Marc Jacobs, who did it
about three years ago." Pearson also tells me about Marni, an
Italian house that's being talked about as the new Fendi—
they do sleek, understated coats for the younger, smaller

woman—and about Narciso Rodriguez, the designer of Carolyn Bessette Kennedy's wedding dress, whom Pearson sees as the wave of the future. "Narciso's fur coats are incredibly modern and simple," Pearson says. "Very straight, very unassuming, but gorgeous and beautifully made."

I get my hands on Marni's current collection book and fall in love with a midcalf-length, straight-cut number, black suede on the outside, sheared white Mongolian lamb inside ($5,000). But when I go to Saks Fur Salon, which carries Marni and a lot of other designer furs (Dolce & Gabbana, Fendi's medium-priced line, Birger-Christensen, Ferré), they don't have the Marni I'm looking for. I try on about 17,000 others, including a sea-foam-green squirrel, a stenciled "pony" (don't panic, it's really calfskin), and a Fendi medium-priced-line, Mongolian lamb–trimmed suede coat, which looks sort of like the Marni and reverses to become a raincoat. That one costs $4,800, but the Mongolian lamb fur is long (not sheared), and it swallows me. After an hour of this, I'm thoroughly confused. Will I ever find the fur for me?

Over lunch with my friend Gabriella, I learn something new. She says that you can sometimes buy designer furs directly from the manufacturer, at substantial savings. Why didn't I know this? After a little judicious scouting, I go to see Anne Dee Goldin, a third-generation furrier at Goldin-

Feldman, the top-of-the-line manufacturer that has made coats for Yves Saint Laurent, Chloé, Geoffrey Beene, and others, and does it today for Guy LaRoche and Narciso Rodriguez. It was Anne Dee who had the insight to persuade Narciso to do his own line. She shows me the whole range of Narciso's inventions, nearly all of which are reversible and feather-light: a tiny shirt jacket with side slits that's blue-black (he calls it "ink") suede on one side and blue-black Persian lamb on the other; a three-button, V-neck mink cardigan that reverses to tobacco suede; a midthigh-length camel suede jacket with a hood (the other side is gray Persian lamb); an adorable knee-length straight mink car coat, with a collar, that reverses to aubergine suede. (Would it be as wonderful if it were called eggplant?) Prices range from $4,000 for the shirt jacket to $30,000 for an Alaskan sable coat (which I don't even look at). The coats are all in odd lengths. They're casual, sporty, unstuffy, and delectable, and unlike anything else I've seen. My two favorites are a tiny funnel-collar ink suede Persian lamb jacket and the mink car coat ($9,000), both of which I try on about a dozen times. I feel I'm getting closer.

I also visit Lawrence Schulman, another third-generation furrier, whose firm, Alixandre, works with Oscar de la Renta, Valentino, Yeohlee, Joseph Abboud, and Isaac Mizrahi. Like a lot of people in the fur business, Larry is a charmer and a fashion plate; bright red Prada shirt and tie, gray double-breasted Cerruti suit. After finding out what I'm looking for and what I can spend, he brings out a full-length, straight-and-narrow natural mink by Oscar de la Renta ($19,000). "You need a wardrobe coat," he tells me. "This one is modern, it's chic, it's a functional coat that will keep you warm, and it looks wonderful open. It's a real clean, simple coat." It does look wonderful, but I'm not sure about the big square shoulder pads, and it's too expensive, and it would certainly keep my husband three paces behind me on the street. As a lark, Larry lets me try on a $195,000 full-length Russian sable by Valentino. It's indescribably soft and cuddly. "Charge and send?" he jokes. What about a shearling, I ask? "As a wardrobe coat? If your budget was limited, yes." He brings out a chocolate-brown shearling by Joseph Abboud. This one costs $3,200 and is actually a man's coat, but he wants me to try it on to see how light it feels. I love the way it looks on me, even though it's too big. It's easy, it's comfortable, you can wrap yourself up in it, and it weighs nothing. The construction is minimal. "I'm going to show you something else that's too big for you, but just try it," he says. It's my Marni coat, sheared Mongolian lamb inside and chocolate suede outside, but it's made by Valentino! I love this coat. It's young and warm and cozy, although not nearly as light as Narciso's. He tells me I can get it in ink blue in my size, for about $3,200. This one may be it.

Over the weekend, visiting friends on Long Island, I drop in on Narciso himself in his Wainscott summer rental. He's a short, dark-haired, soft-spoken, boyish thirty-eight-year-old in a black T-shirt, loose black pants, and flip-flops. His recent fifty-piece fur collection is the first he's done under his own name since leaving Cerruti last March, and he's as unpretentious and casual as his designs. "You're a woman like the women I know," he tells me. "On the go. You don't want to get out of the car in a long pooh-pooh mink coat and worry about it dragging in the puddle. You need to whip that coat off the backseat and treat it like your sweater or your leather jacket. You can walk into the Metropolitan Opera with it on the mink side and look totally cool, or you wear it with jeans and a white T-shirt and just rock. That's what it's about."

Well, *yes*. I'm down to the wire. Back to Goldin-Feldman, where I preen around in the aubergine (or eggplant) suede/mink car coat and the funnel-collared Persian lamb short fitted jacket. Over to Alixandre and into Valentino's chocolate suede/sheared Mongolian lamb. It's probably the most flattering look for me, but it does weigh a lot, and I'm hooked on lightness and the wave of the future. Although I still love the vision of the Marni, I haven't been able to see it or try it on. A ruinously expensive compromise pops into my head. I'll get the Joseph Abboud shearling to give to my husband for his birthday and Christmas (and count on his letting me wear it whenever I want). For myself, it's Narciso Rodriguez's mink car coat, which seems to have all of mink's advantages but none of its disadvantages. It's light, it's casual, it's beautifully cut, it makes me feel transcendent, and I can wear it on the eggplant side when I'm with my husband. Who knows? In his new shearling, he may even be willing to walk arm-in-arm with my mink.

I always knew I'd marry a WASP. I grew up in Newport,

Rhode Island, where my grandfather, fresh from Armenia,

landed in 1880 and established himself selling Chinese export

porcelains, objets d'art, and European standards of taste to the new-rich millionaires on Bellevue Avenue. My father, who took over the family business, wore Brooks Brothers suits and could have been mistaken for a governor of the Spouting Rock Beach Association (Bailey's Beach). His younger brother, my uncle Reggie, went to Harvard and then joined that ultra–Ivy League club, the United States Foreign Service. We were so assimilated that I didn't realize the WASP establishment was defunct until I left Newport in the late 1970s and went to live in Washington, D.C. In the end, I did marry a WASP, of course, but not the Newport kind. He grew up in Llewellyn Park, New Jersey, and I wasn't the first non-WASP he'd married; apparently his need to escape the hive was as strong as mine to belong to it.

E. Digby Baltzell, the sociologist who made WASP (White Anglo-Saxon Protestant) a household word, predicted more than thirty years ago that the declining WASP establishment would develop into "a closed caste, protecting its way of life and privileges while gradually abdicating from its position of leadership." I suppose it's my fault that we've been spending some time lately in places where Baltzell's prediction seems right on target, places that my husband calls "WASP hotels." He sees himself on these occasions as a kind of cultural anthropologist, observing the mores of a former ruling class that now functions as an ethnic minority, with rituals that are observed all the more punctiliously because the tribe is so diminished. That's fine with me.

There are, we've found, around a dozen such hotels, in out-of-the-way—and invariably idyllic—waterfront locations, such as Sea Island, Georgia (The Cloister), Mackinac Island, Michigan (The Grand Hotel), Irvington, Virginia (The Tides Inn), and Dixville Notch, New Hampshire (The Balsams). If you're not a WASP, it's very likely that you haven't heard of them, which is just the way they want it. WASP hotels advertise discreetly, if they do so at all, in magazines like *Golf Digest*, and they discourage publicity. Periodic "newsletters" to previous guests are what really carry the message. "It is because of your kind recommendation that we are able to maintain our fine clientele," a typical newsletter advises. Pennie Beach, who runs the Basin Harbor Club on Lake Champlain in Vergennes, Vermont, told me that 65 percent of her guests are return visitors, and that three-quarters of the newcomers learn of the place through word of mouth.

What really sets WASP hotels apart from other establishments, though, are the great and subtle pains that are taken to make sure that their fine clientele is "compatible." When I called the Weekapaug Inn in Weekapaug, Rhode Island, using my maiden name, Kazanjian, I was told that they don't accept reservations for single-night occupancy. On an impulse, I called back under my married name, Mrs. Calvin Tomkins, and mentioned that my husband and I had greatly enjoyed staying at the Gasparilla Inn in Florida (a really ur-WASP place). This time the manager had "a lovely corner room" available for the night we wanted.

WASP hotels act like clubs and sometimes call themselves clubs. Males over twelve years old have to wear ties and jackets after six P.M. Credit cards are not accepted, for the most part, and there's no tipping—a service fee is tacked onto the bill. Meals are American plan, and you get the same table in the dining room each time, and the same waiter or waitress—a trim, blond college student with perky manners and burnished skin. (The heavier young women get to make up your room.) At breakfast, there is a special jam waiter who brings around an assortment of condiments and spoons out your choice; dinner begins with a vegetable server who dispenses ripe and unripe olives, pickled mini-ears of corn, and other crudités. The food is club food, bland and virtually identical from one inn to another. For years, the chef at the Basin Harbor Club (summer season only) spent the winter cooking at the Gasparilla Inn. Most of these hotels are still run by the family that founded them—the Basin Harbor Club was started in 1886 by Ardelia Beach, Pennie's great-aunt—and the same families come back to these places year after year, generation after generation. They bring their children, and later those children bring their children. This is where kids learn to do WASP stuff: sailing, kayaking, tennis, golf, mountain climbing, bird-watching, waterskiing, knot tying, sulking at breakfast.

Here are some things you can expect to find in a WASP hotel: men in green blazers, plaid pants, and tennis hats, and ladies in pastel cardigans and Lily Pulitzer wrap skirts; a TV room instead of a TV in your room; Postum, Jell-O, and coconut macaroons on the menu; wire soap dishes screwed not quite flush to the wall; separate faucets for hot and cold water; framed photographs of early days at the inn going back more than fifty years; at least one golden retriever; green-on-white writing paper and note pads; a croquet pitch; one-speed bicycles; twin beds with mattresses that are either extrafirm or seriously lumpy—one of the keys to the WASP code is a certain degree of planned discomfort. Accommodations, while not exactly a steal, run well below those at luxury resorts; peak season rates range from around $200 to $350 a day per couple, meals and kids under sixteen included. (This year's kids are the next generation of paying guests.) The clientele also likes to economize whenever possible; instead of meeting their friends in the bar, they'll invite them to their room and serve up drinks in toothbrush glasses.

Here are some things you won't find: room service; com-plementary shampoo and conditioner; cappuccino; Jacuzzis; people talking on cell phones (in some places, there isn't even a telephone in your room). Nor will you see bikinis, plunging necklines, or high heels—no sexiness, please, and nothing, absolutely nothing designed by Ralph Lauren. Other no-no's are expensive jewelry, guests sending back their entree to the kitchen because it isn't cooked right, and organized group activities—people in WASP hotels smile and say hello to each other, but nobody *lingers*. A fuzzy, unfocused friendliness hangs in the air. At Weekapaug Inn, where we had our one-night stay, the friendly aura is so pervasive that you don't even get a key to your room, because the doors don't lock.

Last February, when we wanted to get away from the New York ice cap for a few days, the word "Gasparilla" just floated into the conversation. My husband's parents used to stay at the Gasparilla Inn in Boca Grande, Florida, in the 1950s, and I remembered hearing Newport people talk about it when I was growing up, but neither of us knew whether the place was still in business. A telephone call to Boca Grande information proved that it was, and a little offhand use of my husband's family connection worked like an access code. We booked ourselves in for four nights, were duly informed of the necktie-

and-jacket requirement, and learned that payment should be in cash or personal check.

Driving down the coast from the Sarasota airport in our Avis compact, over the little toll bridge that separates Boca Grande from Florida's west coast, it occurred to me that maybe we were making a ghastly mistake. Were we letting ourselves in for four days of intense boredom, among the sort of people my husband goes out of his way to avoid in Newport? (One difference between a Newport WASP and a Llewellyn Park WASP is that the Newport strain snaps the ends off supermarket string beans *before* bringing them to the checkout counter.) Our first view of the inn didn't exactly dispel this anxiety, but there was something deeply reassuring about its appearance: a large yellow wood-frame building with white columns and white wicker furniture on the wide front porch, set back on its quiet street behind a row of coconut palms. The Gasparilla, in short, presided like a benign dowager over its identically appointed yellow-and-white cottages and over the small, well-behaved town of Boca Grande. At the reception desk inside, I saw our name on a list of guests "arriving today" along with Gardiners, Biddles, Coolidges, and other haute WASP coinages. On the way to our ground-floor room, we passed the card room with eight rattan tables, a very small beauty parlor, a large display of seashells behind glass, and a wide, carpeted stairway leading to the other two floors. Our room was big, high-ceilinged, twin-bedded, and proudly devoid of anything that might be considered luxurious. There were flowered chinz curtains, chenille bedspreads, boating prints, two smallish, stiffish towels, and one bar of Caswell Massey pomegranate soap to serve both sink and tub.

For the next three days, wearing proper all-white attire, we played tennis on the impeccable courts of the Gasparilla Beach & Tennis Club, which was a two-minute walk from the inn. We lunched by the pool and napped under thatched umbrellas on the beach, overlooking the placid, blue-green gulf. While I was doing my thirty laps in the narrow lap pool behind the clubhouse, I chanced to overhear parts of a conversation between two substantially proportioned ladies who were doing *their* laps widthwise instead of lengthwise.

"I can't believe it's happening again," said one. "What have I done to deserve it, anyway? . . ."

One lap later, I caught the words "Orthodox wedding" and "religious instruction." I gathered that the first daughter had already married a Jew, and the second was just about to. "He's perfectly nice, of course," she added.

It was not, I think, an exchange that would have offended or even surprised many of the guests. Although the inn will never be guilty of overt anti-Semitism, and the occasional Jewish name may sneak into the guest book from time to time (as a result of a marriage similar to the one being discussed in the lap pool), certain things could be taken for granted here. There were no black people at Gasparilla during our stay, and no Armenians, either. In these surroundings, with my curly dark hair, olive complexion, and mostly black wardrobe, I felt like an *odar,* as my Armenian forebears called people outside the clan. I tended to stick very close to my non-*odar* husband, who couldn't help looking like a WASP in his khakis, his tennis whites, and his worn-out Keds. He even walked like a WASP, something I hadn't noticed until then, with that slightly toed-in, foot-dragging, diffident amble. When I pointed this out to him, he was cross for the next hour.

In the late afternoons we gathered shells, looking for exotic specimens—lion's paw, lace murex, turkey wing, calico scallop, shark's eye—that we'd seen in the inn's front hall display cases and also in Henry Francis Du Pont's collection, which had been amassed over a period of fifty years and donated to the local library. Du Pont's sister Louise was married to Francis Boardman Crowninshield, the Boston social lion, who discovered the place soon after the inn opened in 1912, and who was mainly responsible for bringing in Saltonstalls, Cabots, Lodges, Ameses, Coolidges, and other Boston Brahmins. The early clientele was not exclusively Boston. John Singer Sargent vacationed here, along with various Astors, Drexels, and Wanamakers. J. P. Morgan died here. Lyndon and Lady Bird Johnson were frequent visitors. Jackie came with her mother, Mrs. Hugh D. Auchincloss. Katharine Hepburn came by herself.

The inn's current owner is Bayard Sharp, Henry Du Pont's cousin, without whose approval nothing much gets done in Boca Grande. If you merely rent an apartment or own one of the dreaded condos that have been going up at the other end of the island, you're not allowed to join the Beach Club; only house owners can do that. "They say it's just a bunch of rich people trying to control the island," a gravel-voiced woman at the Beach & Tennis Club told me. "Well, they're right. It is."

Rich, maybe, but not noisy rich or newly rich. The people in Boca Grande (ironically, the words actually mean "big mouth") take their pleasures quietly. Some of them come down mainly for the tarpon fishing in the early spring, and if they're very lucky they get to put their initials on a tarpon scale and hang it in the Pelican Room at the inn. Others play golf. The 48ers Club goes back twenty years, to a week in January when Bayard Sharp invited forty-eight of his best golfing buddies down to fill forty-eight empty rooms. Bird watching is a big draw, and so is the ancient allée of banyan trees on Banyan Street. WASP ladies make a brisk business of shell collecting, carting the better specimens home to be turned into necklaces, earrings, and other ornaments suitable for handmade, cost-effective Christmas presents. Additional activities are porch sitting, canasta, backgammon, going to bed early, and five-course meals.

Oh, my, the meals. Dinner in the long, too-bright dining room, with its floral-patterned carpet and its implacably competent host, Mr. Witham, who never misplaces your name, is a lesson in *autres temps, autres moeurs*. I gaze around the sea of tables, each with its cheerful complement of two or four or sometimes eight well-behaved diners, and I am struck by how much alike the women look. Deeply tanned, more thin than fat, blond, freckled, dressed in the resort clothes of thirty years back, shunning makeup, secure in flat shoes (my four-inch-high yellow Manolo Blahnik mules draw alarmed stares as we are escorted to our table), carrying their accessories in those Nantucket straw bags with the little ivory whale on top. The ladies, no matter what their age, all clearly belong to the same tribe. The gentlemen, God bless them, are the same way: as homogeneous as the overcooked peas on my plate. And every person in the room is relentlessly nice.

"Nice to see you, dearie."

"Nice day."

"Nice tie."

"Nice game."

"Am I like that?" my husband asked me anxiously, on our last evening at the Gasparilla. "Is that me in ten years?"

"Of course not," I reassured him. "Don't be silly. You're deracinated."

He gave me a funny look. It was clear that we would not be coming back. It was also clear that I was feeling ridiculously at home.

W hy a woman would wear a black dress is a total mystery

to me." Bill Blass, a favorite designer for the super-rich,

sounds genuinely perplexed. "Doesn't it bore you always to

put on black clothes?"

It does, to tell the truth. I've been wedded to basic black for most of my adult life, for all the obvious reasons—it's easier, it's New York, and I think it makes me look taller and thinner. Lately, though, I've begun to have doubts. My friend Eric, never at a loss for a compliment, recently told me *again* to stop looking like a Sicilian widow. Besides, I keep hearing these rumors that color is the next big thing in fashion, that it's about to roar in the front door and chase the little black dress out the service entrance. As far as Bill Blass is concerned, this is not news.

"My observation is that rich women never wore black to begin with," he tells me.

"Only us working types?"

"Absolutely. Black is a classless color. But women with money, who have huge wardrobes and change their clothes two or three times a day—and believe me, there are still plenty who do—they don't wear black. I simply don't understand why you can't experiment. You don't have to have every color that a rich woman has in her wardrobe, but color makes you feel better, and it's also more attractive to men. Start with a jacket, or a little vest. A bright emerald green or a red. It doesn't matter. Just get it. Try something."

All right, already, but before I take such a life-threatening plunge, I feel as though I should find out what a few other trendsetters have to say about the current rage for color. Donna Karan, who designs with the working girl in mind, has never strayed too far from the neutral basics: black, beige, gray, navy. There's very little color in her new fall line, but when I ask her whether color is coming in, she says, "It's starting. For spring I'm doing tons of color. I am definitely exploring the possibilities of color."

Which colors? "Pretty yellows. Palm green, a eucalyptus kind of green. Greens are my favorites because they look very similar to khaki and neutral. I started playing last spring with what I call emotional colors—blues, greenish blues. No brights, except as an accent here or there." Karan's idea about color is more restrained than Bill Blass's, and she certainly hasn't abandoned black. "Black will never be gone," she says. "Black is always there, white is always there, neutral is always there. In New York, black is a way of life; it's a foundation. And then you can add color."

What a relief. My foundation can stay. I have an idea. Not wanting to rush into things, I go to the back of a closet—not my closet, but a storage closet in my mother's house in Newport—and pull out an Yves Saint Laurent coatdress that I got in 1986. It's sleeveless and has large, bright red, purple, and pink poppies on a white ground. (I bought it in a daring mood and wore it once.) A week later, with some trepidation, I wear it out to lunch in New York. I definitely feel different in it. Highly visible, for one thing, but also, I must confess, years younger, and, well, pretty. Two construction workers give me the full, 180-degree ogle, something that hasn't happened in quite a while. Vesna, the maîtresse d' at Petaluma, claps her hands and says, "How fifties!" When I come home, the Bolivian woman who works for us, whose English is limited, greets me by saying, "Mees, you look Barbie." I don't know about this color stuff. If it's a choice between a Sicilian widow and Barbie, I'll take Palermo.

Better still, I'll call Isaac. Isaac Mizrahi knows everything and shares it readily. "Color is in," says Isaac. "I'm definitely making that statement. Color is for everybody. Even people like you who wear only black are starting to wear color now. Color means that you're passionate about something, that you're vulnerable and passionate and expressing yourself.

"Right now, gray is selling in place of black. This medium, gorgeous, Tippi Hedren pale gray worn with pink, with pale, pale yellow, with scarlet. There's nothing more beautiful than red and gray, is there? At all? Geranium red and gray. Right? Perfect. But the biggest-selling thing in my collection this fall, I am not kidding, is this hand-knitted aquamarine cashmere twin sweater set. You have to have that, sweetie. You have to have that with a gray skirt or a black skirt."

Isaac did his sweater sets in six shades, which he calls "soup colors." "It's like you took aquamarine and made soup out of it, but it's not pastel. It's got a lit-from-within quality because of the amount of white in it." The other colors include orange, "bright, bright, bright pink," a very pale yellow, and an intense grape. What Isaac really doesn't like is "that horrible politician blue. Women think it looks great on TV, but it doesn't. It's revolting. It's just the most awful color."

Mizrahi is not into the sort of bright, one-color power suits that stigmatized the 80s. Fashion is much more relaxed now, he says, and inappropriateness is in. "When was the last time you saw a Chanel suit that looked like a Chanel suit? The chicest people I know today are wearing pull-on pants—Indian pull-on pants in fatigue green, let's say. And some amazing little pastel T-shirt in a luxurious fabric. A friend of mine had a dinner party the other night, and she wore velvet. Red crushed-velvet pajama pants and a little black halter. In August! I thought, You are such a genius. Individuality is in, which is why it's impossible to say one group of colors is in and another isn't. I'll just say that the customer I design for feels that it's young to wear color now. It's just young. It's aging to be this black widow every time somebody sees you, you know? You gotta get a life, Dodie. You have to open *up*."

Listening to these three designers, I get the message:

Color right now is in the accessories and accents but not necessarily the main event. Bill Blass told me not to think about a daytime dress or a pant in anything but a neutral color; Donna Karan said more or less the same thing, and Isaac Mizrahi was talking about "a bit of color here and a bit of color there." That makes it a little less daunting and a little more doable. I need another opinion, though, and since my last recorded dip into color—two bathing suits in 1988, one citron and the other bright red—happened at Norma Kamali, she's the one I turn to. Norma Kamali, who used to have hair as dark as mine, is now a fiery redhead. "To be honest with you," she says, "when I did my hair red, it got me into thinking about color. Because look what happens." She goes over and puts her head next to a blue sweater on a rack. Wow. I see what she means, but Norma Kamali generates two thousand volts of primary color without even trying. I'm afraid my voltage is somewhat lower.

As I look around the store, though, what hits my eye mainly are blacks, browns, and grays. "There's a whole new gray thing that everybody is doing," Norma tells me. "I've developed a palette of grays that have color in them—blues and deep violets and browns. For spring, I'm using lots of color, but I'm using it to complement strong neutrals that have color in them. I tell you, I really am in such a mood to do color."

How does it happen that everybody is in such a mood to do color, all at the same time? I've often wondered how these things get decided. Is there some sort of designer conspiracy? Do they have top-secret conferences in the Himalayas? In any event, I'm stuck with the old dilemma: Color may make me look too rich, but it certainly won't make me look too thin. Norma Kamali concedes that most of her customers are still clamoring for black, mainly for that reason. "Black does give the illusion of a thinner line," she says. "However, there are other things that do that. There are things that color can do to balance body issues. Color can make you look prettier; it can give you a younger, more vibrant look. Since I did my hair red, everybody tells me I look like a kid."

What about bright color, I ask her. "I'm hoping that people will be brave enough for that soon. The impression is still that people who are not savvy about fashion wear bright colors. That may not come until the millennium, not before we get into the feeling of a new time. We're going through a very chaotic time now, so maybe it will take a bit longer to see color worn with happiness."

If color equates with happiness, though, why not wear it?

Norma Kamali's new line is 100 percent polyester jersey—sounds retro, but it's wrinkle-free, not too clingy, machine washable, lightweight, great for traveling, and actually has a good feel. I try on a three-quarter-length riding jacket in bright red (just like my bathing suit), which, to my surprise, I love. It has two patch pockets that work, and no buttons. Kamali recommends that I wear it with a gray jersey pull-on pant and a sleeveless V-neck top in the same bright red. "In the most perverse way, red is still a neutral," she says. "I could see you in a little red dress, to the knee. But this red jacket becomes your neutral jacket that you could put over black dresses or pants. Think about it. If you feel ready, if you're excited about it, you're going to look great in red because you'll wear it with confidence. But if there's the least bit of fear or doubt, don't do it."

I also try on a long jersey shirt that buttons up the front. She makes it in three lengths—the one I put on comes to my ankles. It's in one of her color-infused grays, somewhere between deep violet and blue. I can wear it open, like a coat, over a pant or a skirt, or even a bathing suit, or I can wear it buttoned as a sleek, slimming shirtdress. This is something I could really go for.

On the way out, my eye catches a mannequin in what Kamali calls her "bubble skirt," short, knitted, and very full.

I love it, but I couldn't possibly wear it, I say—too young for me. "Oh, stop it," she chides. "Get your hair colored and come back. Go and see Victoria at Bumble & Bumble. You should do a little piece of it, a strip or a section, in dark navy or blueberry. You'd look amazing, I'm not kidding." A blueberry strip? *Moi?* Would that boost my voltage or just blow a fuse?

Two days later, believe it or not, I'm in Victoria Hunter's chair at Bumble & Bumble. "Norma Kamali said a blueberry strip would be great for me," I venture.

"She's a little trick, isn't she?" says Victoria, the Australian-born supercolorist to the supermodels. "Tell Norma to stick to clothes. I'd like to see your hair more broken up." She talks about softening my dark brown hair by mixing in pieces of lighter brown and chestnut red. "You have a lot of thick hair, and I'd like to make it more three-dimensional rather than one solid color."

I think about that on the way downtown. Passing the Seagram Building on Park Avenue, I drink in the big, bright yellow Tony Smith sculpture, *Light Up*, out front. It does wonders for Mies van der Rohe's dark brown masterpiece. No doubt about it, color does lift the spirit.

But am I up to the challenge? The whole idea makes me nervous. Is there an artificial conspiracy against black, or is the tide really turning? In spite of my doubts, I'm taking the plunge. My all-black closet is in for a shock. My hair is in the process of becoming 3-D: dark brown, lighter brown, and chestnut red. I'm getting two cashmere sweater sets in Isaac's "soup colors"—one in aquamarine and one in orange—and I can't resist Norma's red riding jacket. After that, who knows? I might even learn how to be inappropriate with confidence.

The Body

I t was the dead of winter. My regular exercise studio had

folded, my chronic stiff neck was getting worse, and I was

feeling tired, pettish, and generally crummy. Time for a

change. In New York, that usually means a new exercise

program, but not necessarily one as drastically different as SuperSlow, which I heard about from my colleague at *Vogue*, Charles Gandee. "It's not recreational—this is much more like going to a shrink," he told me. "The price of admission is that it's blindingly painful." Hmmm. Charles is over six feet tall, and through SuperSlow he's gained thirty pounds of "absolute muscle." That's hardly what I have in mind. But I happen to know that Mary Boone, who's about my height and my age, is also a SuperSlow devotee, and when I saw her at one of Leo Castelli's many eighty-ninth birthday parties, I was struck by how terrific she looked.

SuperSlow—the very word sounds un-American—contradicts almost every current theory about exercise. Forget aerobics, whose benefits are unprovable and which may even be counterproductive (i.e., strained muscles, torn ligaments, et cetera). What SuperSlow offers are twenty- to thirty-minute sessions of intense, focused muscle-development exercises, performed at an excruciatingly slow speed and only twice a week. Working the muscles in this way does everything that aerobics is supposed to do for the cardiovascular system, but does it more efficiently and without the risks—that's the claim, anyway. Finding a certified SuperSlow trainer, though, can be a problem. There are only two hundred of them in this country, and not a single SuperSlow facility in Manhattan. Gandee put me on to his trainer, Jim Clarry, one of the rising stars in the SuperSlow movement—he has trained everyone from Mary Boone to Calvin Klein to RuPaul—and I started working with him last December, at the uptown, all-purpose David Barton Gym on Madison Avenue.

I have to admit I was a little apprehensive about a male trainer, but that vanished after five minutes with Jim. He's a tall, slim, soft-spoken, gentle young man whose quiet confidence is immediately reassuring. At our first meeting, we talk for forty-five minutes, sitting on the long bench by the windows, while the aerobics-mad clientele pump and sweat and pedal away at the shiny machines on all sides. "I want you to get really skillful at a few exercises rather than moderately skillful at many," he says. "There's a learning curve. We can't get to exercising until I teach you how to exercise. SuperSlow cuts to the truth. We're going to strip away everything that's not productive. It all comes down to fatiguing muscles efficiently and then allowing them to adapt to that level of fatigue."

The basic element in SuperSlow technique is the ten-five interval: ten seconds to lift the weight and five seconds to lower it. As Jim explains, this is hard work and no fun. By gradually increasing the weights, he will "inroad" my muscles (get deeply into them) and make them work until they fail; failure, in fact, is the goal of each exercise.

"My objective is putting more muscle on people," Jim tells me. But do I want that? I'm short and sort of frail, at least in my own mind, and I certainly don't fancy being short and bulky. "Bulk is usually due to a combination of muscle and body fat," he says. "If someone achieves a bulky look while training this way, she's probably overeating. A pound of muscle is much smaller than a pound of fat." So, what about diet? "SuperSlow's stance on diet is that there is no such thing as health food and no such thing as junk food. If you eat a hundred apples, you'll get sick." He tells me that I'm not overweight, and that I should keep right on eating the way I have been. The emphasis here is all on the muscles. If we do right by them, everything else—heart rate, energy level, strength, and even the right shape—will fall into place.

Question-and-answer period is over, and we go to the day's first exercise, the stiff-legged dead lift. Jim places two five-pound dumbbells on the floor, positions me precisely over them, has me bend at the waist without flexing my knees, and tells me to lift the weights very slowly, to the count of ten seconds, and then lower them in five. I do this eight times, keeping my knees stiff. It exercises the hamstrings, glutes, and back muscles, all the way up to the spinal erectors at the base of the neck, he explains. Nobody has ever worked on my spinal muscles before; I didn't even know I had them. Aside from a slight tingling in my lower back, I don't feel much of anything, because the weights are too light. Today's session is just to learn the motor skills. He teaches me three more exercises—leg press, chest press, and weight-assisted chin-up—one with free weights and the other two on Nautilus-type machines. The protocol is to repeat each exercise four to eight times; if you can do eight repetitions, the weight gets increased. I do eight of each exercise without much difficulty. The pain is yet to come.

My learning curve continues through the first few sessions. I'm going three times a week, and Jim keeps adding exercises and increasing the weights. Five days after Christmas, we're up to eight exercises, which is the most we'll ever do at one time. I'm lifting a thirty-five-pound dumbbell for the stiff-legged dead lift and moving 146 pounds on the leg press. We go rapidly from one exercise to the next, and I notice that my heart rate stays elevated the whole time. "It just so happens that during SuperSlow your heart rate is elevated to what you would achieve on a treadmill or stationary bike, which is what's recommended in cardiovascular training," Jim tells me. Doing the chest press today, I have my first failure—seven repetitions is all I can manage. "Keep pushing, keep pushing," he says, as I struggle, lying flat on my back, to lift the ten-pound weights in each hand. "Keep it there for another twenty seconds. Try not to lose any ground. This is the most important time. We need to fail." My heart is racing, my whole body is trembling. The pain is so severe that I feel dizzy. After what seems like two lifetimes, Jim takes the weights out of my hands and says, "Good work." This is what I have to look forward to on all the exercises: to succeed by failing.

By this time I've learned a little more about SuperSlow theory and practice. It was developed in the early 1980s by Ken Hutchins, who until then had been working closely with the inventor of the Nautilus machines, Arthur Jones. Hutchins broke with Jones over the issue of aerobics, which he saw as a wholly misguided approach to fitness. Instead of the frantic activity of the aerobicists, he put his faith in slow, concentrated, precisely measured stressing of the muscles. The slow part of SuperSlow makes the lifting much more difficult but also much safer. "The most dangerous thing you can do while exercising is apply too much force to a joint," Jim tells me. "Force is mainly a product of speed and acceleration, and we're eliminating most of that. And remember, the goal is to fatigue the muscle, not to lift the weight." All around us, the treadmills and stationary bikes are going full tilt. Jim says he has nothing against treadmills; "it's just that people think they're burning off more calories than they really are. The machine tells them they're burning off about two hundred calories an hour, but they'd be burning off a hundred calories just sitting on a couch." In other words, they're wasting their time. Jim's advice is that I can jog or play tennis or go to body-sculpting class if I want, but I should do it for fun, not for exercise.

It's now three weeks since I started the program, and I'm coming to failure with more and more of the exercises. Washing my hair in the shower this morning, I noticed something astonishing—biceps! Neat little biceps, not a bit like Arnold Schwarzenegger's. And my stiff neck is totally gone. One of the exercises we do each time has me lying prone on a narrow bench and slowly raising my head while Jim exerts a counter-pressure with his hands. And unlike the other remedies I've tried over the last year, including Motrin, prednisone, and physical therapy, it works. Jim says I'm making great progress. He no longer has to remind me to breathe regularly during exercise; "val salva," or holding your breath, is a definite no-no, and so are the grunts and clenched teeth that often precede it. (There's plenty of grunting and groaning in the David Barton Gym. There isn't any in a proper SuperSlow environment, which has white walls, no mirrors, no music, no telephones, no gum chewing, no bimbos, a constant sixty-one-degree temperature, and a metronome for the ten-five beat.) I've also learned to keep my movements smooth and constant, with no jump starts or pauses in between. "Don't save anything," Jim keeps saying each time I approach failure. "Whittle away at it. You can do it."

There's surprisingly little soreness between our sessions, although, according to Jim, this is neither good nor bad. The sessions are getting shorter and shorter. We're down to thirty minutes, because my skills have increased, along with the weights, and I'm coming to failure more quickly. Out on the street after a workout, my body feels like molasses. The legs are moving and the upper body is going with them. It's exhilarating to feel so good and energetic.

Lunch with Ann Piccirillo, my former exercise teacher, the one who slimmed down my thighs with light "focus" weights and a draconian diet that took away bread, pasta, and carbonated beverages. (She closed her Manhattan Body studio last year to write a book about *her* exercise technique.) When I tell her what I'm doing, she's horrified. Lifting a fifty-five-pound dumbbell (as I did this morning) without bending my knees is lunacy, she says. "You never, ever, lift something without bending your knees." I'd always heard that, too, but it doesn't seem to have done me any harm. Ann also says that using heavy weights is going to bulk me up. She offers to give me the name of a good therapist and a good acupuncturist, because she's sure I'm going to need them if I go any farther with this.

The part about bulking up really worries me. The other night I asked Charles Gaines, whose book and film *Pumping Iron* set Arnold Schwarzenegger on the road to stardom, whether lifting heavy weights makes you bulky, and he said, "Yes, definitely." I raise the question again with Jim Clarry at our next meeting. I say I don't want to look like the muscle-bound bruiser in the "before and after" photographs in the SuperSlow manual, which I had borrowed from him. Not to worry, he says. "The guy in that picture was eating seven thousand calories a day, and he's genetically gifted—something very few people are." He reminds me that muscle mass is smaller than fat mass and says that I definitely will not bulk up from using heavy weights. Besides, having always been a ninety-nine-pound weakling, I can use a little extra on top, and that should make my hips and thighs look slimmer. But what about the lunacy of lifting that dumbbell without bending my knees? As long as I do it slowly, Jim says, there's no risk.

We're into February now. I'm still going three times a week and making progress. A couple of problems have come up, which Jim has dealt with swiftly and effectively. I was waking up with severe chest pains. Jim thought they might be caused by the chest pad I lean into on the rowing machine; he took me off that machine, and the pains faded away. An old pain in my left hip kicked up when I was doing abduction exercises on a leg machine. Instead of taking me off that machine, he added an adductor machine that reversed the motion, and the problem cleared up. He wants me to develop callouses on both hands to strengthen my grip. I hate that idea, so he finds me a pair of padded exercise gloves. Jim listens very carefully and knows his subject through and through. "He's the most informed and rigorous trainer I've ever met," Mary Boone tells me. "If he ever started his own gym, I'd put money in it." Mary also says that she and I are both dealing with the same problems, age and gravity. "And we're not going to find a plastic surgeon who will make us six feet tall."

In March I'm failing at everything. My leg press is up to 240 pounds. I get nauseated every time I do it, and my ears are stopped up, as if I'm riding in a fast elevator. All the exercises make me feel this way now, but often I can think beyond the pain and feel my way more deeply into the muscles. "Don't acknowledge the pain," Jim says. "When you acknowledge it, it hurts more. It's like having your hand over a flame—you want to pull it away, but here you make yourself keep it there. Exactly the opposite of what human nature teaches you. No compromise." Several people have told me I look great. On a trip to Los Angeles, I see myself in a mirror at the Beverly Wilshire and think maybe it's true. My proportions look better, the hips and thighs slimmer, the shoulders a little wider.

On April 11, I can't do a single leg press. It's time to cut me back from three to two sessions a week, Jim says. I've gotten so good at it that I've overworked my muscles, and they need more time to recover. "One of the drawbacks of aerobics is that people don't give their muscles time to recover, and that makes them weaker, not stronger," he says. "Most people work out too often but not hard enough." With SuperSlow, the better you get, the less frequently you do it. Twice a week is the preferred schedule for SuperSlow. (The really good SS-ers do it once a week, but some of Jim's trainees hate to cut back.) In place of my third session the next week, I take a long walk in Central Park with my husband, not for the exercise but for the fun of it. We climb the steps to Belvedere Castle and check out the early spring flowers in the Shakespeare Garden.

A whole new prospect is opening up for me. Ever since I was sixteen, I've had a compulsion to do some sort of exercise every day. If I didn't, I'd feel guilty. But now I can get all the exercise I need in two twenty-minute sessions a week (maybe one, eventually) and have that much more time for doing the things I like. My stiff neck is gone, my thighs are as slim as they're ever going to be, I haven't bulked up (it seems I'm not genetically gifted, thank God), and I show off my biceps at the drop of a hat. I actually feel stronger, healthier, and less tired. Is the blinding pain that goes with those two sessions a week worth it? I'd say it is. There are moments when I even feel six feet tall.

Long Hair

A year and a half ago, I had my hair cut really short—

about an inch or so all around. At the time, I thought it was

farewell to long hair. I'm in my forties, and somewhere in the

back of my mind was the notion that age thirty-five was the

cutoff point (no pun intended) for long hair. But I missed my hair, missed being able to braid it or ponytail it or just wind it around my finger in idle moments, and so I let it grow again, to the point where it's now right back where it started, two or three inches below the collarbone. This made me feel like a backslider, until I learned, just recently, that there was an epidemic of long hair on the runways for the spring collections. Almost all the supermodels showed up with silky, shiny, pancake-flat hair down to the waist or lower, and the jet-set ingenues-who-count quickly followed suit. Long hair, very long hair, much longer than mine, is suddenly de rigueur. How did this happen, and where does it leave me?

Everybody knows you can't grow hair like that overnight. There has clearly been a big run on extensions, falls, and other additives, so I decide to go out to Cedarhurst, Long Island, to see Rodolfo Valentin, a leading designer of high-end hairpieces. Rodolfo is six-three, Argentine-born, flamboyant, and no more burdened with modesty than his near-namesake, Rudolph Valentino. His shoulder-length black hair goes awfully well with his black boots, black jeans, and black velvet shirt unbuttoned to the waist. "I do plastic surgery with hair," says Rodolfo, whose business has doubled in the last year. As we speak, he is bonding twelve-inch-long strands of hair to a customer's head with silicon, seven strands at a time, row on row. "I sell to the biggest salons in Manhattan. I do royalty in Europe, movie stars in South America. I love hair. The day I die, I would like no flowers, just lots of hair, hair, hair."

Rodolfo makes ponytails that come in three lengths, from eight inches to two feet long. He makes clip-on bangs, falls that are attached to headbands, and "umbrellas" to add fullness. He uses only real hair, every hair going the same way, root to end, and he buys only the best. "Italian hair is supposed to be the top," he tells me. Next to Italian, he likes hair from Spain. Sweden and the Nordic countries provide his blond hair. He doesn't much like Asian hair, because it's "too heavy, too thick individually, and very weak," but hair from India is fine, "thin and strong." Blond hair is more expensive than brown, of course: Blond ponytails run from $800 to $3,000; his brunette ones from $700 to $2,900. I ask him about my hair—could it be longer? "Absolutely. It will be a sophisticated look for you to have very long hair, but with a limit, probably not more than six inches longer." Six inches would come down below my breasts. Could I really do that? "You have a young look, and your long hair is helping you." Intrigued but not convinced, I arrange to borrow one of his two-foot-long ponytails and carry it home in a little pink box.

At nine the next morning, I'm at Garren New York Salon, the hair salon at Henri Bendel. Garren does Linda Evangelista and other superheads, and he also does the suburban matron in from Peapack. His clothes are as black as Rodolfo's, but his manner is cool, low-key, and gentle. "I would say fifty percent of my clients now have long hair," he says. "There's no age limit to long hair. That old saying that after thirty-five you've got to cut your hair—no! That's the worst time to do it. A lot of women, if they cut their hair off, become matronly." (Even Julia Roberts, according to Garren, looked a little matronly when she cut hers.) Garren says that the right hair length is a matter of body type and attitude. "There are longhaired girls, and then there are women who just don't know how to handle long hair. A longhaired girl really has her gestures and her movements working together, but someone who's uncomfortable with long hair keeps tucking it behind her ears all the time." He says it's important to keep long hair away from your face—headbands are okay as long as they're understated and subtle—and to keep the neck area clean, without a lot of jewelry or fur collars. He gives me an appraising look. "Your hair is long, and it works for you, because you're a longhaired girl. But I think it would be ridiculous if your hair was breast-length. Yours should not be the long that we're showing for spring. It has to do with proportion. You're very narrow in the shoulders [I wish he'd said hips], your face is tiny, and the superlong hair would just drag you down, es-

pecially because your hair is dark. Anything past your collarbone is wrong. I'd like to take an inch and a half off your
length and redefine the front a little bit."

My plan had been just to run around and talk with some
hair gurus, but when I visit the John Barrett Salon at Bergdorf
Goodman that same afternoon, Barrett puts me right in the
chair and goes to work. (I guess he can't bear to let me leave
looking the way I do.) He gets Christopher Cilione, one of his
top colorists, to enliven my near-black hair with some precisely placed, ultra-subtle brown highlights. Then he enlists
Denise Chaplin to clean up my eyebrows. ("Eyebrows are crucial to the new long hair," says Barrett. "We have to get that
right.") Finally, he joins the fray and starts cutting. Barrett
takes off about an inch and a half (exactly what Garren had
recommended), cutting a slight V into the back part "just to
soften it up" and get rid of the "squareness." No shaping, no
layering, but a very big-deal blow-dry, with assistance from
Dawn and Zack.

"I'm seeing more long hair than ever," Barrett tells me as
he works. "It's possible for just about anyone to have long
hair, if you've got the right cut and the right conditioning and
particularly the right color. That long, flat hair that we saw on
the runways is too impractical for most women. But look at
[socialite] Lyn Revson, with hair down to her waist. The color,

the conditioning, and the cut are done impeccably. It's couture hair, expensive hair. The extraordinary thing we're seeing now is this really clean, pure look, with very little makeup. What we want to do is replicate beautiful-child hair. The style influences are coming more out of Hollywood than Milan or Paris. There's a younger crowd of women like Gwyneth Paltrow with beautifully straight, beautifully conditioned hair, parted down the middle and held back away from the face, sometimes with barrettes. It's very glossy and very healthy and really luxurious. It's not contrived hair, and I don't think it's age restrictive." For anyone over eighteen, though, it's high maintenance and very expensive. By the time Barrett finishes with me, I'm late for dinner. But my new "childlike" hair feels wonderfully light and silky, and it actually gets noticed by Edmund and Sylvia, with whom I'm dining. "I like the way it moves," says Edmund.

A lot of Steven Dillon's customers are not coming in as often for haircuts these days, because they're growing their hair long. Steven Dillon, of the Brad Johns Salon, is twenty-nine, a former actor, and a rising star in the hairdressing heavens: He tends the increasingly long manes of the three blond Miller sisters, Aerin Lauder, and other young dazzlers who love his signature look of "very clean, undone, sexy hair," as he describes it, hair that looks "like you just got out of bed."

Superlong hair is definitely a trend, he tells me, but "I don't think everybody can wear it. If you're forty, you shouldn't have hair down to the waist, unless you're Cher or Madonna. But I don't think it's just an age issue. It depends on a lot of things, including what you do for a living." Who shouldn't wear long hair? I ask him. Pastry cooks and women with short necks, for starters. Also, "people with really fine hair, or over-processed hair, or too much makeup. People who are short and petite shouldn't wear superlong hair. It just doesn't look good; it overwhelms them." Count me out for superlong—I'm small and already overwhelmed.

"Stand up," he commands. He studies my head and body from various angles. "You could wear it longer. I think you could pull it off, but your ideal length is probably where you are now, or a little bit shorter. I'd just make a few adjustments around the face, to make it a little sexier and a little less droopy. Your hair is amazingly healthy and shiny for someone blowing it out all the time." (I don't tell him that this is courtesy of John Barrett's all-out conditioning treatment the day before.) What about extensions? "Extensions are great, but they can ruin your hair. The hair breaks off completely. Healthy hair is a must. You have to have healthy hair to have long hair. You have to condition it all the time. I use a treatment creme called Phyto 7—it's my savior in a bottle. You should wash your hair once a week, and not a lot of blow-drying."

Dillon has a bevy of impatient customers in the cutting room, but he plops me down in one of his six chairs. "You're not leaving here without a haircut," he says. "You need a little bit more of an edgy look—not funky but sexy. Hair to me is sex." He snips away, taking out John Barrett's V. "I can see you've been to John Barrett," he says. "Yep. We're un-Barretting you. I think a straight line in back is much more what's happening now." In the front, he cuts rapidly back and forth, layering and pointing a few strands at a time in graduated lengths from nose to chin, creating infinite variations on a sleek yet deliberately imperfect theme. He has me stand up again while he slides the edge of the scissors to taper the ends. "Details, details," he says. "It's the difference between a Mercedes and a Volkswagen. I guarantee that this will be better than any haircut you've ever had in your life."

He's right about that. My hair has never felt so pleased with itself. It moves fluidly, it shines, it has a life of its own that just happens to conform perfectly with mine. That same evening, I pull it back, plug in Rodolfo's ponytail, and go to a dinner dance, where my friend Eric stops me short by saying I look like Juliette Gréco. Like who? "Juliette Gréco," he says.

"That singer who was the toast of Paris when Sartre was holding court at the Café de Flore." I think this is a compliment.

There's one thing I still have to do, which is to check in with Kenneth, the perennial monarch of coiffure. "Let's have a spoonful of reality here," says Kenneth. "I have nothing against these twelve-year-olds on the runways, or eighteen-year-olds, with waist-length straight hair. If you're willing, and have the hair to do it, and the patience and the looks, then do it, for Christ's sake. But not because *Vogue* says so. I don't care about what's in or out. You've got to look in the mirror and decide who you are and what makes you look best. I don't say that older people can't have long hair; they just can't wear it straight down around their face. The law of gravity doesn't permit it. You've got to get your hair back from your face at a certain age—I don't care if the length is at your waist or not."

So where are we? A spoonful of reality can seem like a bucket of cold water, but Kenneth is infallible. When I look in the mirror, I don't see a potential Lady Godiva or Rapunzel. I can see a two-foot ponytail for cotillions, but my borrowed one has to go back to Rodolfo, alas. What's left is the hair length I've had most of my life, but this new model looks and feels more like a Mercedes than a Volkswagen, and I'm hoping to get a lot of mileage out of it. Like most men, my husband prefers long hair, and he loves the John Barrett color highlights and the perfectly done-undone look of Steven Dillon's cut. In the end, it's farewell to short hair for me, and probably a lot more time at the hairdresser. But I'll think about that tomorrow.

Note: Steven Dillon left Brad Johns in the spring of 1999 and is now at the Pierre Michel Salon.

Lipstick

How can it be that I've never worn lipstick? Here I am in

my prime, living in Manhattan, working for *Vogue*, and still

wearing Vaseline on my lips for every occasion. The other day

I learned that 92 percent of American women use lipstick

regularly, 6.2 days of the week. So what's my problem? It was my kid brother, Powel, who used to tease me about having "monkey lips." Or maybe it was just a case of not wanting to grow up; wearing lipstick, after all, is what little girls do when they want to be big girls. In my teens, I began using a bit of eye pencil, and I've been doing that ever since. But I never wanted to call attention to my lips with color. About two months ago, however, it occurred to me that this might be my last chance—unless I try lipstick now, I probably never will.

Lipstick now is such a vast and polyglot subject, though, that I hardly know where to begin. Do I want matte or creme? Lip gloss or sheer? Stain, shimmer, shimmy, or shake? Thousands of colors are out there, from divinely decadent greens and blues to whispery nudes to all-out Jezebel scarlets, in a range of prices from $1.99 at the local Duane Reade to $22.00 at Chanel, and a range of durability from Long-Lasting to Transfer Resistant to Smear Proof. More and more makeup artists put out their own special lines, which compete with such familiar giants as Estée Lauder, Revlon, and Lancôme. And the names! Just Bitten, Baby Lips, Mystique, Philosophy, Mischief, Slink, Naked, Prophecy, Fudge, Kiss Me Red, Rizzo (after Ratso?), Plain Truth. They come in tubes, pots, wands, pencils, bottles, and, for all I know, shoulder holsters. Finding what's right for me is going to require more than trial and error, I can see.

As a first step, I go to see Laura Mercier at Bendel. Laura Mercier is one of the top makeup artists in the business right now, the wizard of choice for Madonna and other immortals. To my great surprise, she's not a bit scandalized when I tell her I've never worn lipstick. "You have dark hair, dark skin, dark eyes, and you already have color in your lips, so you don't have to automatically put color on top of that," she says, in her pleasantly French-accented voice. "You could go without. But, I think if you wear lipstick, that couldn't hurt." We both laugh. "I used to wear Chapstick a lot when I first moved to America," she adds. "Strawberry Chapstick, Cherry Chapstick. It's a great idea because there is a little bit of pigment in it, but it's not heavy. That's the texture I did when I made what I call my Bitten Lips. The idea is that you get an undertone of a bitten lip, like when you bite your lips and it looks healthy and sensual. I think you could absolutely begin with one of my Bitten Lips colors."

According to Laura, pink lip shades are back in favor for spring and summer, after being non grata for several years. So are lavenders and lilacs and other romantic hues. It's a reaction against "the beige," she says—"all those pale lips and dark smoky eyes, which made everybody look kind of sad." The beige look virtually erased the mouth and accentuated the eyes. Now the mouth is speaking up for itself again. She takes me over to the Laura Mercier makeup counter and sits me on a high stool and says, "Relax, be calm. You have the right to not like it, to scream and cry." She outlines my lips with a Chestnut lip pencil and then starts filling in with Just Bitten. "When I created my line, at the very beginning, Just Bitten was *my* color," she says.

"Laura, you can't call it Just Bitten anymore." Danielle Devine, who handles Mercier public relations, has arrived just in time to correct her. Apparently there has been a legal dustup with Estée Lauder, which makes a lipstick called Bite Your Lips; as a result, Mercier's Just Bitten is now called Just Lips. More bark than bite here, I'd say.

Laura says that she would love to try a red on me, because she thinks I could "definitely" wear it. Strong reds have never gone out of favor, of course; red lipstick, like the poor, is always with us. "But you will feel overwhelmed with red at first, you will feel strange, you will feel that everybody is looking at your lips." We agree that I'm not ready for red yet. But I love the way Just Bitten (Oops! Just Lips) looks on me. My lips are basically the same color they always were, but fresher looking and more distinct. She also gives me a tube of Baby Lips, pinker than Just Lips and a great favorite of Madonna's.

Walking home on Fifth Avenue, even though I'm not wearing red, I have the impression that people are looking at my lips. But I feel more polished and grown up. My lips are a little dry, though, because they're used to Vaseline. Over a lunch of crackers and cheese and Diet Coke, I taste lipstick and I see lipstick marks on my glass. Yuck. That evening, before going out to dinner, I reapply my Just Lips. It looks awfully dark in the tube, but on my mouth, the effect is so subtle that at first my husband doesn't notice the difference. When he does, he seems pleased, even though he always says he doesn't like lipstick. (Could that be one of the reasons I married him?) At dinner, two people tell me I look great, not something I've been hearing so often lately. Hmmm.

The next morning, I visit Bobbi Brown, another top-notch makeup artist, whose popular line of cosmetics is now owned by Estée Lauder. Bobbi is vivacious, dark haired, pregnant, and fun to talk with. Her personal clients include Susan Sarandon, Brooke Shields, and Winona Ryder; Hillary Clinton wears her No. 16 Tea Rose pink lipstick, and Dennis Rodman comes in regularly for her No. 5 Bronze Shimmer. "I'm the perfect person for you," she tells me, when I explain my lipstick virginity. "I started my company because I looked so terrible in lipstick. I have a very small mouth. The first thing I designed was lipstick. They're pinky browns. I think brown lipstick is really ugly, that dark muddy purple. But something a little pinky just wakes up your whole face. My biggest tip with lipstick is to find one that works when you have no other makeup on."

She starts me off with Bare Stain. Stains are the cool thing right now, and this is one of her lightest shades. "I think you want noncommittal makeup," she says. "You can't make a mistake with this color." To me, it looks as noncommittal as Laura Mercier's Just Lips, which is fine. "You have a full mouth," she says approvingly, "so I don't know why you hate lipstick." I don't hate lipstick. It's just that I have this anti-deluvian thing about calling attention to my mouth. I've always felt that the eyes and the mouth were in competition, and that in my case, the eyes always had it. The eyes are supposed to reflect the mind, the soul, and the higher emotions; the mouth is sensuality and appetite. Virginia Woolf vs. D. H. Lawrence—not that I see myself as a card-carrying intellectual. But it's true, I do have a full mouth, and right now I'm putting on Bobbi Brown's Nude matte lipstick. It's a smoother, creamier version of Bare Stain, and my husband, who can't stand obvious-looking lipstick, would definitely not like it. After considerable blotting and wiping, I try Cranberry Stain, which she says was Carolyn Bessette Kennedy's favorite. She directs me to put it just on my lower lip, and then smack my lips together. Not bad. I can see myself wearing this for a black-tie evening. The stain lipsticks last longer than the sheers, but not as long as the current flock of "indelibles," which are big sellers on the mass market right now. "Every single company has these twelve-hour lipsticks," Bobbi says. "They look terrible for twelve hours. I think lipstick should come off and go on again." Neither Laura Mercier nor Bobbi Brown make long-lasting lipsticks. Bobbi sends me off with a kit that includes the lipsticks we tried on and several others, plus her lip balm, which she says is an essential preparation for all of them—you put it on first, wait ten minutes, and then add color. Before I leave, she drops a little secret. If she doesn't have her balm handy, she uses Aquaphor, "the stuff that's used on babies' bottoms."

One of my good friends who wears lipstick all the time because "it makes any woman look better," complains that she's never been able to find a lipstick that really lasts. That night, after talking with Bobbi Brown, I dreamed I put on one of the twelve-hour lipsticks, a blazing red, but it turned out to be mislabeled. It was a twelve-*year* lipstick, and nothing I tried—even paint remover—would take it off. I was branded, sentenced to bright red lips for the next decade, a scarlet woman.

The next day at the Chanel counter at Bergdorf, an Asian saleswoman who's seriously weighed down with matte brown lipstick produces four tubes for me: Rose Cinder, Pink Sugar, Pink Accent, and Mischief. I test them on the back of my left hand (to avoid germs) and ask to see others. I pull out Lilac, which is a Hydra Soleil (their most transparent lipstick), but the saleswoman says, rather impatiently, that it's not for me. "I've shown you what's best for you. Which ones are you going to get?" I tell her I haven't decided which one. "One? Do you know how many lipsticks I own? Two hundred! Go for the Mischief. It's new and it will look good on you." Mischief is a creme lipstick; I ask if it's as translucent as the Hydra Soleils, but she's already ringing it up, for $22.00. "You got the best one," she snaps, "so be happy with it."

Donna, at Bloomingdale's Chanel counter, couldn't be more helpful. Although she's wearing Mischief herself, she says it's not for me—"much too opaque and much too much color for you to start off with." (She's absolutely right, as I discover when I get home.) She doesn't think Lilac is for me either, but I can't resist the fresh, springlike look of it. When I try Lilac that evening, it glides on as though it belongs there, with no sense of intrusion. Chanel, as usual, is a world apart for me—the squared-off black and gold tube, the lipstick's smooth feel, the delicate, supertransparent hue all combine to make me feel pampered, sophisticated, transformed. For the first time, I sense that this is something I could really get hooked on.

Over the next few days, I test-drive a whole galaxy of lip products by Poppy, M.A.C., Prescriptives, Face Stockholm, Guerlain, Shiseido, and Philosophy. (That's right, Philosophy. Any day now, they'll bring out Kierkegaard and Wittgenstein.) Everywhere I go, I get the impression that sheers, stains, and glosses are in the ascendance, while mattes and creams are in retreat, along with hard-edged pencil outlining. I buy a lot of noncommittal lip glosses, as well as a number of lip balms and vitamin E sticks, which to me are the real revelations. I've abandoned Vaseline for Aquaphor, and I'm experimenting with Face Stockholm's Vitamin E stick, Chanel's Maximum Moisture Lip Treatment, and Bobbi Brown's Balm for big nights out. (Laura Mercier has just brought out her own mineral stick, called Lip Glacé—it comes in raspberry, cocoa, champagne, and crystal. I can't wait to try it.) The balms are my new accessories, and I'll never leave home without them. I've also acquired a respectable lipstick wardrobe (or arsenal). It includes Shiseido's Blackberry Gloss (there's a permanent waiting list for this one) and Philosophy's Supernaturals, a liquid tint that makes me look as though I've just finished eating a bowl of raspberries—it comes in a tiny bottle, along with a tube of lacquer, which I don't use because it makes my lips stick together. Also, M.A.C.'s Rizzo (the name still puzzles me), a delicate pink that would be perfect for an outdoor summer lunch party; Guerlain's deliciously subtle Rose Nenuphar (that's water lily), and its brand-new Orange Tropical, which reminds me of the orange frosted lipstick that my mother unfailingly wore to the beach. I like the idea of wearing orange, which has been out of fashion for ages.

And then there's red. My husband used to think that lipsticks came only in red. Can you picture Man Ray's painting of two huge female lips against the sky *(Observatory Time: The Lovers)* in Brown Shimmer? Laura Mercier said that I could definitely wear red, when I was ready for it, and once again, I think it has to be now or never. I have to try it, and I decide to go all the way with Paloma Picasso's Mon Rouge, the only color she wears or makes. (Paloma Picasso started wearing red lipstick at the age of three.) Mon Rouge comes in a hefty gold tube that's autographed and refillable, but I won't be refilling it. As I put it on, I see myself turning into a predatory avenger in the mirror, and I nearly scare the pants off my husband. To calm him down (and me too), I go back and replace it with a discreet application of Chanel's Moisture stick.

The curtain falls for seven days, as Ring Lardner once put it, to denote the passing of a week. And the truth of the matter is, after all my experimenting, I've decided that lipstick and I just don't get along. It's absurd, I know. I'm condemning myself to a permanent membership in an 8 percent minority that's made up primarily of librarians, telephone linewomen, and nuns. But my Chanel Maximum Moisture stick is a big improvement over the Vaseline jar, and when I pull out that signature squared-off black and gold tube in a restaurant (no mirror, of course) and apply it with airy sophistication, I bet people think I'm just like the rest of you.

Calming me down

I f you wouldn't hesitate to take a hot shower, you have nothing to worry about with kava." Chris Kilham, a leading evangelist, developer, and promoter of the hottest new herbal medicine since Saint-John's-Wort, is reassuring me on the phone. I've had a bottle of kava-root extract on my bedside table for six weeks, but I've been afraid to try it. I'm not a pill popper, I get insomnia from decaf coffee, and the whole idea of herbal cures makes me anxious. Anxiety, though, is the very thing that kava is supposed to alleviate. And this just happens to be shaping up as a day chock-full of anxious-making pressures. "Why don't you take two this afternoon at four o'clock," Kilham cheerfully suggests. "What about one right now?" I propose. No problem. He tells me to take it on an empty stomach, with half a glass of water, and, somewhat to my surprise, I up and do it, at ten twenty-one A.M.

At ten-thirty, Sueli, my irresistibly friendly cleaning lady, arrives and starts talking to me while I'm trying to interview another kava expert on the phone. (One of the perils of working at home.) A messenger buzzes me from downstairs—our doorman doesn't come on until three P.M. I can hear my husband coughing as he waters the plants out on the terrace; he's supposed to be sick in bed, but he won't stay there. The buzzer rings again. This time it's Clotaire, the lab technician who comes once a week to draw blood from my invalid mother. I give up and cut short my telephone interview. While Clotaire is drawing blood, I put in a call to Authentic Refinishing, the firm that's promised to send someone here by ten to recondition our bathtub. My other phone rings. I put Authentic on hold. It's the Democratic party calling to ask for money and, for all I know, sympathy—no, please. By the time I get back to Authentic, the receptionist has hung up, and then, for the next five minutes, the line is busy. It's now ten forty-five. Maybe I'm imagining this, but I don't seem to be going out of my mind as I normally do on days like this. In fact, I feel relaxed, content, and even sort of happy—just the way kava is supposed to make you feel.

What exactly is kava? I had done some research before actually trying it and learned that it is an extract from the plant *Piper methysticum,* a member of the pepper family, which has provided comfort and considerable pleasure to South Pacific islanders for more than three thousand years. Captain James Cook brought it back from Polynesia in 1777. Pope John Paul II, Queen Elizabeth II, and Hillary Rodham Clinton (I) drank it on ceremonial occasions in Fiji and Hawaii. Now, riding the tsunami of "natural" medicine that is making herbal supplements a multi-billion-dollar industry, kava has suddenly, within the last year or so, become an over-the-counter superstar. The kava market here has zoomed from virtually nothing in 1994 to nearly thirty-five million dollars last year. Although the Food and Drug Administration forbids suppliers to advertise it as a treatment for anxiety, this is exactly what Chris Kilham and quite a few doctors who specialize in alternative medicine say it is. Kava is to anxiety, they claim, what Saint-John's-Wort is to depression: a safe, natural, nonaddictive alternative to Valium, Halcion, and other pharmaceuticals, with none of the harmful side effects. According to Harold H. Bloomfield, M.D., a respected psychiatrist who has written on kava and other herbs, "Researchers are not yet sure exactly how kava works," but it seems to have a soothing effect on the amygdala, the brain's alarm system.

Clearly a lot of people are convinced. But I wasn't. My hesitation about trying it, though, was not just skepticism and natural timidity. The *New England Journal of Medicine* warned in its September 17, 1998, issue that some people have become severely ill from herbal supplements and urged that this loosely regulated industry be held more accountable for its products. Kava was not implicated in the *Journal*'s reports, and the studies that have been done on it in Europe, though too narrowly based to be conclusive, show it has no addictive or adverse side effects if taken in moderate doses over a short period time. (A more extensive placebo-controlled kava study is currently in progress at Duke University Medical Center.) My own doctor didn't know about kava. He had no objection to my trying it, but he wasn't enthusiastic. With prescription drugs, he said, you know what you're getting, but with supplements—which aren't monitored by the FDA—you don't. He told me about a report in which fifteen out of thirty brands of a particular supplement were tested and found to have none of that supplement in them at all. Still, in spite of my ingrained skepticism about roots and herbs, I was curious about kava, curious enough to hunt some down.

Clayton & Edward Chemists, my regular pharmacy, didn't have kava and seemed vague about what it was. I tried the local Duane Reade, and the pharmacist there told me to go to The Vitamin Shoppe or General Nutrition Center, because (surprising candor), "The ones that are stocked in big pharmacies are not really as well made." At The Vitamin Shoppe, the salesman asked if I wanted it in capsule or liquid form. The liquid tastes awful, I'd heard, so I opted for capsules— but what kind? He brought out the house brand. "Is that the best?" I asked. He said yes. Unconvinced, I left and tried my local health-food store. "We have many brands of kava, and they're all just as good," the proprietor said, beaming. Finding the right kava, it seemed, could be as stressful as shopping for a Chanel suit.

Next stop, the "all-natural" Hickey Chemists, whose proprietor, Jerry Hickey, is chairman of the Society of Natural Pharmacy. Mr. Hickey explained to me that whatever kava brand I buy should be "standardized," which means that it should have 30 percent kavalactone (the active ingredient in kava) per 200- to 250-milligram capsule. He recommended the Mariposa brand, which wasn't on the market yet—he was expecting it in a week or so; pending its arrival, he suggested Natrol Kavatrol ($10.36 for thirty capsules) and told me to take one capsule three times a day, with food, adding that it would take "a couple of weeks to kick in."

A couple of weeks? With food? Matters seemed to be getting more and more complicated, not to mention anxiety provoking. Later that day, I talked to Ronald Hoffman, M.D., a nutrition expert and host of the nationally syndicated radio show *Health Talk.* He assured me that kava works immediately, requires no buildup in your system, and can be taken on an as-needed basis for mild anxiety or tension.

"The pharmacists confuse it with antidepressants like Saint-John's-Wort, which takes about two to three weeks to work," he said. "Kava is not an antidepressant. It's not even a sedative, because it doesn't knock you out. It just has a relaxing effect. The other night I took four because I felt particularly revved up after my radio show, and I wanted to calm down. I was sitting outside on my balcony listening to a little music, and suddenly felt, what a wonderful night. Temperature just right, so peaceful, the lights so beautiful. I just felt pretty good."

Hoffman does not recommend kava for clinical anxiety, like panic disorder or social phobia. "Kava is good for everyday anxiety," he told me. "But if you're having panic disorder with this surge of adrenaline, it's not going to do any good."

Finally, we're getting somewhere. I liked the idea of being able to take it on an ad hoc basis, especially since reading that overdosing on kava can lead to "a scaly eruption or yellowing of the skin," something I always try hard to avoid. The scaly eruptions, it turned out, have been observed only in rare cases of Polynesians drinking many bowls of liquid kava every day for several months. I also learned that kava should not be taken by people with Parkinson's disease (it might worsen muscle weakness), or if you're pregnant or planning to become pregnant (because its effect on the fetus is uncertain). Nor should it be combined with alcohol or pharmaceutical antidepressants, tranquilizers, or sleeping pills (it could temporarily knock you out). But for healthy people who take a standardized brand in moderate doses over a short term—a pill or two, three or four times a week—there appear to be no side effects. So what was I waiting for?

Before taking the kava leap, I talked to Samuel Benjamin, M.D., a disciple of top health guru Andrew Weil, M.D., and the director of the Center of Complementary and Alternative Medicine at SUNY Stony Brook. "Kava is a really intriguing drug," he told me. "It has a lot of potential use, because it's not addictive. It has a place as a *very* short-term-use tranquilizer for *some* people, for mild anxiety. But let me tell you the problem. Ain't no drug that's not going to cause problems when you take it for a long time, and kava is a drug. People think it isn't, because it grows naturally, but arsenic also grows naturally. We have this fascination in the United States with anything that's natural. And we are an abusive society. My concern is with the people who believe that this is the way to respond to problems they can't address."

Dr. Benjamin went on to say that kava does not seem to alter mental clarity, as the benzodiazepines (like Valium and Halcion) do, but "because it has a sedative-*like* action, it should not be used when driving or operating machinery of any kind." Dr. Benjamin is certainly not anti–herbal medicine. He has practiced alternative medicine for twenty-eight years, and he believes strongly in the importance of herbal products when used properly. They're a lot cheaper than prescription drugs, and he feels that people should have them as an option—but only if they have the right information. "I don't believe in health-food stores," he said. "I was in a health-food store a few days ago, and this kid behind the counter, a high school kid, was giving advice to an elderly lady who was shaking from Parkinson's disease. He was reading out of a book and telling her what vitamins to get. These people practice medicine without a license. This should be done by pharmacists."

Most of the people I talked to agreed on the need for more regulation of the booming herbal-supplement business, but even Dr. Benjamin told me to go ahead and try kava. "You could use it for three or four days, a couple of times a day," he said. "If you're about to interview Prince Charles, and you're anxious about it, fine."

I'm not likely to interview Prince Charles, but I did end up trying kava: the Sundown brand—large, manure-colored capsules with a pungent reek. I've taken it once about a week ago (as I mentioned), and felt good for the rest of the day.

Science demands further tests, though, so this time I try a different brand. Chris Kilham recommends KavaPure ($15.95 for thirty), which he considers the best on the market. He also likes Sundown, which comes from the same extract and is readily available at drugstores. "If it's good kava, you feel it within twenty minutes," Kilham says. "Kava is unique in that sense. Just like if you have a good cup of fully caffeinated coffee in the morning, all of a sudden you feel perked up." But kava doesn't work like java. "If you have trouble going to sleep," Kilham says, "kava relaxes the muscles and quiets the mind. It doesn't actually make you sleepy, but it will help you sleep, and it will also give you a more refreshing sleep."

It sounds like kava will do anything you ask it to do. Maybe I can get away with just rubbing the bottle? But what the heck. I bite the bullet and try it again, KavaPure this time, one soft gel cap at eleven P.M. I'm in bed, my thoughts are racing, and sleep seems very far away. I start reading F. Scott Fitzgerald's *Tender Is the Night,* and believe it or not, within fifteen minutes, things start to seem more tender. My interior voices pipe down, my pulse slows, I'm on the French Riviera, on that "bright tan prayer rug of a beach" in front of Gausse's Hôtel. Fitzgerald's limpid prose plays its part, of course, but there's also a sense of well-being that's extraliterary. I read for about an hour and a half, totally absorbed, and then sink into the most completely satisfying sleep I've had in years.

Some things I dream about having

A garden by landscape architect Dan Kiley

Menshikov chocolates from Chartres

Fluency in French

An Issey Miyake scarf

Pretty much anything from Treillage, the fabulous New York garden furniture and offbeat treasures emporium

Manolo Blahnik mules for every occasion

A Richard Benson clock that runs for ten thousand years

Undersize white note cards from Cartier engraved with pale blue lettering in Cartier's own typeface

A ceramic sculpture by Peter Schlessinger

One of Robert Rauschenberg's silkscreen paintings from the 1960s

A small cottage overlooking the ocean in Newport (pure fantasy—it doesn't exist)

A first edition of Jane Austen's *Persuasion*

Seventeenth-century oversize French table silver from the Paris flea market

The most comfortable stuffed armchair in the world for reading

A gold wire-and-crystal necklace by Kazuko

Drawings from Cecily Brown's 1995 film *Four Letter Heaven*

Nothing less than business-class travel from now on

Alabaster and jade frogs for finger bowls

A potting shed/greenhouse filled with herbs for my finger bowls

An endless supply of rose soaps and essences from Parfumerie Fragonard in Grasse

A nineteenth-century iron Dutch Caribbean canopy bed with its original yellow paint

Time to read all the books I've put aside

A black crocodile belt (not too thick and not too thin) with a discreet silver buckle from J. P. Tod's. (Manolo says it's p.c., "because crocodiles are mean")

Two weeks off to do the grand tour of Piero della Francesca's frescoes in Arezzo and Sansepolcro, with stops in Perugia, Assisi, Urbino, and Monterchi

Lots and lots of Susan Rowland's quirky, one-of-a-kind clay jugs

A small French wooden treasure chest (circa 1800), painted blue with yellow and white flowers, as a sort of spirit-catcher for future dreaming